CULTURE SHOCK!

Egypt

Susan L. Wilson

Graphic Arts Center Publishing Company
Portland, Oregon

In the same series

Australia	India	Singapore	London at Your Door
Bolivia	Indonesia	South Africa	Paris at Your Door
Borneo	Ireland	Spain	Rome at Your Door
Britain	Israel	Sri Lanka	
Burma	Italy	Sweden	A Globe-Trotter's Guide
California	Japan	Switzerland	A Parent's Guide
Canada	Korea	Syria	A Student's Guide
Chile	Laos	Taiwan	A Traveller's Medical Guide
China	Malaysia	Thailand	A Wife's Guide
Cuba	Mauritius	Turkey	Living and Working Abroad
Czech	Mexico	UAE	Working Holidays Abroad
Republic	Morocco	USA	
Denmark	Nepal	USA—The	
France	Netherlands	South	
Germany	Norway	Vietnam	
Greece	Pakistan		
Hong Kong	Philippines		

Illustrations by TRIGG
Photographs by Susan L. Wilson

© 1998 Times Editions Pte Ltd
Reprinted 1998

This book is published by special
arrangement with Times Editions Pte Ltd
Times Centre, 1 New Industrial Road, Singapore 536196
International Standard Book Number 1-55868-401-8
Library of Congress Catalog Number 97-074478
Graphic Arts Center Publishing Company
P.O. Box 10306 • Portland, Oregon 97296-0306 • (503) 226-2402

Printed in Singapore

For Edward and Darrell

Above: View of Elephantine Island in Aswan.

Below: The Red Sea Coast is rugged and scenic – it also has a very good highway.

CONTENTS

INTRODUCTION

Just the word "Egypt" brings to mind visions of pyramids, grand temples, gigantic monuments, mummies, and king-gods, all relics of one of the oldest civilizations in the world. To many, it will forever be the "land of the Pharaohs," a place where agriculture and advanced mathematics developed. But the long reign of the Pharaohs and grand monuments passed away nearly 2,000 years ago. Many facets of life in Egypt have changed, and changed a lot, since the time when grand temples and statues were built to worship its king-gods.

Egypt (formally the Arab Republic of Egypt) identifies itself as an Arab nation (the official language is Arabic, though English and French are also commonly spoken). Its people are "Arabized" rather than true Arabs. The capital city is Cairo or al-Qahirah (el-KA-heh-rah). Egypt covers 1,002,071 square kilometers or 386,900 square miles. It is about the size of Ontario in Canada or the size of Texas, Arkansas, and Oklahoma combined in the United States.

Today, Egypt is a developing north African country of over 60,000,000 people facing difficult challenges as it moves into the

21st century. Egypt is a land of proud, honorable families – each trying to do the same things families do everywhere within the confines of their government, religion, and values. Like people everywhere, they concern themselves with love and having their children grow up to be "good" people. At the same time, Egypt's government must find ways to combat crime, rampant poverty, urban overcrowding, and some very difficult environmental problems.

As humans, each of us, whether in the government or the average person on the street, faces the world within the confines of our culture (that complex mixture of beliefs, behaviors, and societal rules which tell us what is right and wrong, good and bad). Hopefully, this book will bring greater understanding of Egyptian culture: of who modern Egyptians are, how they view life from their cultural perspective, and how they go about facing challenges in a rapidly changing world. In the words of modern Egyptians: *Ahlan wa sahlan!* (AH-lan was-AH-lan) Welcome! You are welcomed to Egypt!

Chapter One

A TOUR OF EGYPT

Egypt is an incongruous mixture of old and new. Considering that Egypt has one of the oldest civilizations known to the world and that it is home to the last standing Seven Wonders of the Ancient World, it is not surprising that just the word Egypt fascinates and intrigues people. Looking around Egypt, one minute you think you have walked through a time-warp straight into Biblical times. Ten minutes later, you may find yourself negotiating a high stakes deal in an ultramodern meeting room, teeming with skilled entrepreneurs dressed in the latest European fashion. Intertwined with remnants of time-worn lifestyles, Egypt is a nation seeking its place in a modern world of computers, telecommunications, and banking. Lifestyles are so intermixed that it is difficult to define where one lifestyle ends and another begins. A booming tourist industry that introduces Egyptians to the world adds another dimension to the amalgam of lifestyles. While many Egyptians remain insulated from direct contact with outside forces, few are far from its influence. Most tourists remain somewhat isolated from real Egyptian life. They stay principally in modern facilities away from the poverty and exhausted infrastructure. Rarely do tourists experience the everyday struggles to move into the "modern" age that affects the lives of Egypt's more than 63 million people.

The modern Arab Republic of Egypt identifies itself as an Arab nation, though its people are "Arabized" rather than true Arabs. The distinction between Arab and Egyptian is well recognized among Egyptians and Arabs alike. Egypt perceives its role in the development of the Middle East as one of leadership, peacemaker, and negotiator. Egypt's rich educational heritage gives it a valuable export – skilled labor. Many Egyptian professionals, doctors, nurses, engineers, teachers, and agricultural specialists work in other Arab countries. They make significant contributions to development throughout the Arab world and bolster Egypt's economy by sending wages back home.

In the following chapters, I will try to add order to seeming inconsistencies in Egyptian life. First, however, we must lay the groundwork by briefly describing the country, giving a few statistics, and pointing out some of Egypt's most pressing developmental concerns.

GEOGRAPHY AND NATURAL RESOURCES

Egypt is located on the far northeast corner of the African continent. It is about the size of Texas, Arkansas, and Oklahoma, combined, or 1,002,071 square kilometers (386,900 square miles). Egypt provides the gateway connecting the African continent with the huge Eurasian landmass. It controls the strategically and economically important Suez Canal and Sinai Peninsula. The Mediterranean Sea marks the northern boundary of Egypt. The Gaza Strip, Israel, and the Red Sea border it on the east; the Sudan stretches from the southern border; and Libya lies west of Egypt's borders.

Egypt is a vast desert plateau interrupted by the Nile River valley and delta. Topographically, it is almost entirely desolate, with barren hills and mountains in the east and along the Nile. The Western Desert comprises slightly over two-thirds of the nation. The Sinai Peninsula and the Eastern Desert add another six and twenty-three percent, respectively, to the desert landscape. The result is that less than four percent of the total area is in the arable Nile Valley and Delta. When viewed with this perspective, it is easy to see why Herodotus so aptly noted in the fifth century BC that Egypt is the "gift of the Nile." Like an emerald green ribbon, the Nile flows 550 miles (880 km) from Egypt's southern border with Sudan, through its desert heartland to the Mediterranean bringing life to an otherwise desert wilderness. The Nile forms at Khartoum, Sudan, when the Blue Nile and White Nile (whose sources are deep in Africa) converge. It separates the Western (Libyan) Desert from the Eastern (Arabian) Desert. As a result of its unique geographical configuration, most Egyptians live in the Delta and along the narrow irrigated strip on either side of the Nile.

Another prominent geographical feature is Lake Nasser, an artificial lake resulting from construction of the Aswan High Dam. Historically, the Nile flooded annually, depositing needed silt all along the Nile's path. Whether Egypt had a high or low flood year depended on rainfall in other parts of Africa. Early in the 1900s, the first Aswan Dam (now below the High Dam) was completed to try to control annual flooding. It was subsequently raised, but still could not control the Nile's raging floodwaters. Only after completion of the Aswan High Dam in the 1970s was the Nile finally tamed. The High Dam was built not only to control flooding, but to increase arable land and generate electricity to facilitate Egypt's move toward modernity. Considerable international controversy resulted from the former Soviet Union's financing of the dam after refusal by Western institutions. The Dam became operational in 1971 and by 1974 revenues had exceeded construction costs. Subsequently, increasing costs of recla-

Traditional irrigation methods included the use of water wheels, like the one shown here, to lift water to crop fields. Donkeys and camels are still used as beasts of burden.

mation have offset the value of providing a regulated flow of Nile water for irrigation.

Though ecologically controversial for several reasons, the High Dam rapidly increased modernization throughout Egypt by providing an accessible source for electrical generation. People will tell you that food just doesn't taste as good as it used to when Nile soil was deposited every year. Culturally, construction of the dam was also controversial. As a result of rising water in Lake Nasser, numerous small Nubian villages had to be relocated north of the dam. Historians and archaeologists worldwide were up in arms because many ancient ruins could not be saved from the rising waters. Seemingly superhuman international efforts saved some historical sites by rapid excavations or by systematically disassembling, moving, and reconstructing them at a new site, such as the great temple at Abu Simbel. Increasing desertification and prolonged droughts in the Sahel and Sahara

Deserts seriously threaten Egyptian water management and use of its water resources. In 1987, Lake Nasser's water level was at its lowest since the lake filled – at a level actually below the amount needed to run the Aswan power station.

Oil and natural gas are two of Egypt's most important natural resources although their quantities do not compare with the high reserves of their neighbors on the Arabian Peninsula. Proven reserves are estimated to be some 6.2 billion barrels of oil with some 500 cubic meters of natural gas reserves. Recent oil discoveries in the Gulf of Suez and the Western Desert suggest these figures will increase. Production of natural gas is sufficient to meet domestic needs and provides a surplus for export. Egypt's other natural resources include iron ore, phosphates, manganese, limestone, gypsum, talc, asbestos, lead, and zinc.

ENVIRONMENTAL ISSUES

Egypt's environmental problems revolve around a rapidly increasing population, poverty, ignorance, and historic lack of concern for environmental integrity. The current government is seeking measures to clean up Egypt's massive environmental problems, but many traditions are deeply ingrained and the existing infrastructure is severely in need of modernization, so progress is extremely slow. Experimental projects look for new ways to maintain environmental integrity while allowing for productive growth.

Of course, the fact that much of the land is effectively uninhabitable presents other environmental challenges – like how to develop sustainable desert reclamation. On top of this, add the fact that the little agricultural land that does exist throughout the country is being lost to urbanization. Oil pollution and new tourist sites along the Red Sea threaten Egypt's coral reefs, beaches, and marine habitats. Natural fresh water resources away from the Nile (the only perennial fresh water source) is very limited although recent underground finds in the Western Desert may provide new sources for limited agricultural development. Agricultural pesticides, raw sewage, and industrial effluents further threaten water supplies.

Natural environmental hazards include earthquakes and occasional flash floods and landslides, along with wind and dust storms. A particularly vicious hot, driving sandstorm, called a *khamsin*, occurs in spring, making the air thick with sand, limiting visibility, and causing breathing difficulties among many.

REGIONS OF EGYPT

For planning purposes, the Egyptian government divided the country into seven major regions: Upper Egypt, Middle Egypt (Assiut); North of Upper Egypt; Greater Cairo; the Canal; Alexandria and Matrouh; and the Delta. Local tradition generally recognizes slightly different regional classifications, so I will stick with local tradition, while recognizing planning needs may require different categories.

Lower Egypt and the Delta

The terms Lower and Upper Egypt, which are used today, have their roots in ancient tradition before the first unification of the two regions of Egypt around 3200 BC. Based on contemporary maps and global logic, one would expect Upper Egypt to be in the north. However, to ancient Egyptians reality revolved around the perceptions of the life-giving Nile whose source lies deep in the heart of the African continent. Since their world revolved around the flow of the Nile, quite logically, Upper Egypt was in the south and Lower Egypt was in the north. These designations are still in use today.

Lower Egypt begins at Cairo and ends at the boundaries of the Mediterranean Sea. Just north of Cairo, the Nile divides into its two tributaries, the Damietta and the Rosetta, forming the huge Delta alluvial floodplain. Extensive networks of canals and channel irrigation provide the Delta area with needed water resources for cultivation. The area provided such high crop yields that in Roman times,

Egypt became known as the "bread basket of the world." Egypt is no longer able to be self-sufficient in its food production. Now, throughout the country, maintenance of high agricultural yields depends heavily on the use of agrochemical products. The larger, more modern farms tend to be located in Lower Egypt. Most of the cotton, for which Egypt is famous, grows in this region.

The moment you leave the Delta proper, you are back in the desert again. Desert extends west from the Delta and eastward, turning into salt marshes along the eastern seacoasts. Desert reclamation farms in Upper Egypt have slightly increased the amount of arable land in the area. Local entrepreneurs have begun developing small fish farms along the shores of the Mediterranean near Port Said. One new corporation, using modern scientific methods, developed an experimental shrimp farm that was quite successful. This ecologically sensitive project, designed to be a long-term sustainable enterprise, is now being expanded to provide a vital new use for salty lowlands.

Upper Egypt

The area from Cairo south to the Sudanese border is called Upper Egypt. The green area from Cairo south is mostly a narrow band of irrigated land along the Nile's shores, rarely extending in breadth for more than a couple of miles. The Western Desert (Libyan Desert) regions of Upper Egypt have begun to experience some development, though progress is slow since most people do not want to leave living by the Nile. In these areas, the government has undertaken several agricultural initiatives to encourage settlement near oases and desert reclamation projects. Farming in Upper Egypt generally tends to be small scale, often family subsistence farming. The landscape of Upper Egypt is dotted all along the Nile with small traditional villages and several small- to medium-sized cities. Large villas, markets, shops, streetlights, several universities, hospitals, and large apartment blocks distinguish the urban areas from the poorer *fellahin* and Nubian villages.

Middle Egypt

Although the whole area from Cairo south is called Upper Egypt, many also recognize a distinction in the center of the country called Middle Egypt. Middle Egypt includes the area around the governorates of Minya, Assiut, and Qena (Qina). However, most people from this area of Egypt also consider themselves to be Upper Egyptians.

Suez Canal

Located at the crossroads of Europe, Asia, and Africa, the Suez Canal is one of the world's most important artificial waterways. It connects the Indian Ocean via the Red Sea and the Gulf of Suez with the Mediterranean Sea. The city of Port Said is located at the northern terminus on the Mediterranean Sea. Ismailia, the administrative headquarters, is about midway through the Canal. The southern terminus is at the city of Suez.

Prior to the peace treaty between Egypt and Israel, the Suez Canal held center stage in several confrontations. The Canal provides the single largest source of foreign currency in Egypt's economy. Going through the Canal shortens the distance from the Far East to Europe by 5,000 miles, thus vitally affecting commercial shipping. Built by French companies starting in 1859, it opened on November 17, 1869. Great Britain acquired the Canal in 1875. Egypt subsequently nationalized it in the 1950s. A sea level artificial waterway with no locks, its total length is 105 miles (169 km) including approach channels. Renovation of the Canal widened its narrowest point to 196 feet and increased its depth to 53 feet to accommodate larger ships.

Sinai and Red Sea

The Sinai Peninsula is the place to go for the newest in Egyptian beach resorts. Other than that, it is mostly a barren desert wilderness with some oil rigs, military outposts, and a few historic sites. It is strategically important because it is the only landbridge connecting Africa with the Eurasian continent and provides the eastern boundary to the Suez Canal. The Sinai is economically important because it contains much of Egypt's proven oil and gas reserves. A few Bedouin (desert nomads) live in the area, but other than that there is little habitation except in the developing tourist villages. Projects are in development to provide a fresh water source for more desert reclamation agriculture. The Red Sea area has beautiful blue-green waters with some of the best scuba diving in the world. Government efforts for national parklands are being implemented to protect some of the more environmentally sensitive areas.

MAJOR CITIES

Cairo (Arabic: al-Qahirah)

Cairo throbs and pulsates with life twenty-four hours a day! Even those of us who like small town living cannot fail to be captivated by her. Teeming with 18-22 million people (and another best guess estimate of 2-4 million daily migrants), Cairo writhes as she strains to burst at the seams. East and west butt each other face-to-face. Few places in the modern world exhibit the inherent clash between the ancient and modern worlds seen in Cairo. Where else can you walk a few blocks from a store selling the newest in information technology to find people keeping goats in their houses? To Egyptians, Cairo is Egypt *(Misr)*, the Mother of the World, and "the victorious."

The site of Egypt's capital (though not the name) can be traced back over 6,000 years. Around 4225 BC, on the western bank of the Nile a few miles north of present-day Cairo, East Delta people built the first capital of a united Egypt. Today, the oldest reminders of ancient Cairo are found in Old Cairo and Fustat (an old garbage dump). In Fustat, known for its pottery production, the air teems with black smoke boiling out of earthen kilns.

Getting oriented to the maze of Cairo is not as difficult as it seems at first glance. First, get yourself a good map and orient yourself to the major sections of the city. Start at the center – Tahrir Square *(Midan Tahrir)* – and work your way out moving clockwise.

North

From Midan Tahrir, go north. Here you will find the neighborhoods of Bulaq and Shubra. When you reach Ramses station, this is the boundary between Bulaq and Shubra. Bulaq was the old industrial center of Cairo, however industrialization subsequently moved northward to Shubra. A very traditional area of Cairo, today's Bulaq is one of the most densely populated districts of Cairo. It is also noteworthy because this area bred much of the recent Islamic unrest.

East

Northeast from Midan Tahrir, you will find Midan Talaat Harb and Ezbekiya Gardens, an area full of Western-style shops and inexpensive, old hotels. Further east, you will find the area known as Islamic Cairo. This area encompasses the Citadel, some of Cairo's poorer districts, and a couple of important medieval neighborhoods. Continuing east and south, you will find the Cities of the Dead. In the Cities of the Dead (huge necropolises), living inhabitants scurry through the vast array of mausoleums rearing children among the funeral vaults. Moving northeast from here, you will reach Heliopolis (where the airport is located), a wealthy district also known as New Cairo.

South

Directly south of Midan Tahrir is Garden City, home to embassies and expensive residences. From Garden City, bridges cross the Nile to Roda Island. On Roda Island you will find Manyal Palace, Cairo University's Faculty of Medicine, the Old and New Qasr al-Eini Hospitals, and the Nilometer. The sprawling suburbs of Old Cairo continue south from Garden City, encompassing the small area known as Coptic Cairo. The next major district moving southward is Maadi. A wealthy district, expatriates tend to congregate in this area.

West

Crossing Al-Tahrir Bridge, you come to Gezira Island in the middle of the Nile. The residential suburb of Gezira occupies the southern part of the island. Gezira is home to Cairo's elite, including some leading diplomats. On the northern half of Gezira Island is Zamalak, another expensive area of town which houses embassies and modern apartment buildings. The famous Gezira Sporting Club connects the two suburbs.

Across the river from Gezira are several districts on the west bank of the Nile. The southernmost district is Giza (home of the Great Pyramids), which stretches to the edge of the desert. Just north of Giza is Doqqi (Dokki). Doqqi houses the rest of Cairo University, and several districts including Imbaba (old home of Cairo's camel market). The camel market has now moved to Birqash about 20 miles (32 km) northwest of the city.

Alexandria (Arabic: al-Iskandariya)

Beautiful Alexandria! After conquering Egypt south to Memphis in 332 BC, Alexander the Great (Iskandar al-Akbar) chose the site of current day Alexandria to be the capital of his empire. What became known as Alexandria was positioned on the west side of the Nile Delta at the site of a small fishing village. Alexandria was envisioned by Alexander to be not only the political and economic center of his empire, but a naval base and great trading port. Alexandria was nearly destroyed when the Arabs captured it in AD 642. An earthquake devastated the famous lighthouse in 1324, another of the Seven Wonders of the Ancient World built on the Island of Pharos in 280 BC.

Alexandria was well designed with streets crossing at right angles. It is wide, stretching some 12 miles (20 km) from west to east. The hub of Alexandria is the Midan Saad Zaghloul, which runs to the waterfront. Just to the east is the Midan Ramla, where Ramla station is located. Alexandria's culture has many distinct Mediterranean influences

The Corniche winds along Alexandria's irregular coastline.

such as in the European quarter as well as its characteristically Egyptian areas. The bulk of Egypt's foreign trade passes through its port. The population of Alexandria currently exceeds two million.

Luxor

Located in Upper Egypt, the contemporary city of Luxor was built on the ancient site of Thebes. Luxor now has a population of around 200,000, most of whom seem to be rather sagacious hawkers and vendors working in the tourist industry. Here modern Egyptians combine an exotic history with modern commercialism. Hordes of foreign visitors walk the streets, even in summer when the heat can definitely be overbearing. What most people think of as Luxor is actually three distinct areas: Luxor city (including Luxor temple), the village of Karnak, and the necropolis of ancient Thebes. The sheer magnitude of Karnak's intricate temple complex boggles the mind. On the west bank of the Nile, directly across from Luxor, the famous Valley of the Kings, Valley of the Queens,

Temple of Hatshepsut, and many finely decorated tombs draw eager tourists anxious to explore the remnants of Egypt's intricate funerary practices. Howard Carter's discovery of King Tutankhamun's (King Tut's) tomb filled with treasures in the 1920s still remains one of the most internationally celebrated sites to visit.

Aswan

Gateway to Africa, frontier city, and prosperous market at the crossroads of the ancient caravan trade route, Aswan is without a doubt one of my favorite places in Egypt. It has a sleepy, almost tranquil atmosphere by comparison to the rest of Egypt. It is here that the Nile is the most enchanting and magical as it weaves through the mass of boulders and small islands, glistening sparkles dancing off its surface. The culture here is different, too – a fascinating mixture of Egyptian and Nubian heritages. Aswan is located on the eastern shores of the Nile about six miles (9.6 km) north of the First Cataract, one of the six major rock outcroppings situated between Aswan and Khartoum.

GOVERNMENT AND JURISDICTIONS

The Permanent Constitution of the Arab Republic of Egypt adopted on September 11, 1971 and amended on May 22, 1980, provides the basis for Egypt's political system and defines public authorities. Egypt's government is a democratic republic with its legal system based on English common law, Islamic law, and Napoleonic codes. According to the Constitution, sovereignty is for the people and they are the source of authority. Egypt has 26 administrative divisions or governorates, each a corporate body. Executive power resides in the chief of state, the president, who may be elected to an unlimited number of six-year terms. The president is nominated by the People's Assembly and then must be validated by a national, popular referendum. The head of the government is the prime minister, who, along with the Cabinet, is appointed by the president.

Legislative authority resides with the People's Assembly *(Majlis al-Cha'b)* which has a total of 454 seats (444 elected and 10 appointed by the president). Under the Constitution, the People's Assembly should not be less than 350 persons, half of whom (at least) should be workers and farmers chosen by direct secret public ballot.

The Advisory Council *(Majlis al-Shura)* functions only in a consultative role. It was formed to widen the participation of intellectuals in shaping the nation's future. The Advisory Council has a total of 264 seats (176 elected and 88 appointed by the president). The Shura is an age-old tradition in Muslim societies.

The Supreme Court and Council of State conduct judicial review. There are three levels of regular criminal courts: primary courts, appeals court, and the Court of Cassation, the final stage of criminal appeals. Since the judicial system is based on Napoleonic tradition, there are no juries. Misdemeanors punishable by imprisonment are heard at the first level by one judge and at the second level by three judges. Felonies, punishable by imprisonment or death, are heard in criminal court by three judges. The Court of Cassation hears contested rulings. If a defendant does not have a lawyer, one is appointed at the court's expense. The judiciary in Egypt is generally credited with conducting fair trials. However, under the Emergency Law, cases involving terrorism and national security may be tried in military or state security courts in which the accused do not receive all the constitutional protections of the judicial system. During 1996, most terrorist cases were referred to Supreme State Security Emergency Courts; high-profile cases involving Muslim Brotherhood members and a large number of terrorists went to military courts.

Egypt's political system is based on a multiparty system within the framework of what is considered "acceptable socially responsible parameters." The National Democratic Party (NDP) is the dominant party. Despite a constitutional ban against religious based parties, the technically illegal Muslim Brotherhood constitutes a significant influence.

ECONOMY

Egypt's principal sources of revenue are from the Suez Canal, agriculture, textiles, food processing, tourism, chemicals, petroleum, construction, cement and metals. Tourism passed petroleum as the second largest hard currency earner in 1995. The complexities of the Egyptian economy cannot be addressed in a few paragraphs. Some things in Egypt seem to be changing rapidly and others at a very, very slow rate. Due to dynamic economic development policies, I hesitate to put hard figures into a discussion of the economy. Rather, I will give you the government's stated economic reform strategy along with highlights of a few characteristics that affect economic development.

Egypt's economy is in the process of liberalization in an effort to transfer the national economy from the governmental sector to the private sector through guided central planning. A number of steps have been introduced to open the economy to encourage growth. Over the past five years, the government enacted significant economic reforms which have reduced the budget deficit, stabilized the exchange rate, reduced inflation and interest rates significantly, and built up substantial reserves. The government undertook several steps to grow the economy in recent years. For example, passage of decree number 95 of 1992 organized the stock market and streamlined procedures for foreign investors, including the granting of residency permission for six months until projects are registered. A centralized authority to streamline company incorporation procedures was also established. Privatization efforts continue to move Egypt away from a centralized economy. Encouraged by the government's privatization program, the Egyptian Stock Exchange (ESE) ended 1996 nearly 40% up on the year, leading all Middle Eastern stock exchanges. Foreign investments increased significantly and by early 1997 Egypt's Standard and Poor's ratings improved substantially.

Egypt has a tradition of entrepreneurship and capital markets, but shifted to a socialized, government run economy in the 1950s. Centralization affected the population in many ways; however a healthy entrepreneur class continued within the constructs of a planned central economy. In this sense, the shift back to a market driven economy would seem to be an easy one. However, the mass of the population was (and is) dependent on elements of a planned economy. The government's economic strategy is to introduce a gradual change program in measured stages. It is not considered a practical or real option to hastily shift to a liberalized economy. Therefore, Egypt adopted a policy of economic reform based on several characteristics that include some very important real practicalities. The comprehensiveness of the plan not only considers the need for economic changes, but also the social and political dimensions associated with all economic sectors. They are quite aware that sustainable economic growth must be accompanied by sustained social stability or they may lose everything.

To many middle- and lower-income Egyptians, the transition seems especially slow. These groups often realize only the immediate results of inflation and a slowly responding job market. Agriculture is the largest employer in the economy and is almost entirely in private hands. Egypt's oversized bureaucracy employs some one third of the population's workforce through government jobs, public sector enterprises, and the armed forces. Privately owned service and manufacturing enterprises account for roughly another 20%; the remaining labor force is unemployed.

Many skilled laborers work abroad (at least 2.5 million) or are underemployed in Egypt. In talking with middle-class, university educated young Egyptians, many claim they are unable to find work in their chosen professions. Often people will tell you that although the government promises a job after graduation from a university, a person must sometimes wait seven or eight years to actually get a job. As a result, the tourism sector harbors large numbers of the highly educated who are unable to find work elsewhere. Consequently, don't be surprised to find a tour guide who graduated law school, but cannot practice law due to the high costs of establishing a practice. Alternatively, you may find an accountant or schoolteacher working in tourism as secondary employment to raise their family income. Most commonly, among the middle- and lower-classes, you will find people working two or three types of jobs to try to make ends meet. In spite of significant actions taken by government which have increased per capita income, the overwhelming majority of Egyptians still live in poverty.

TOURISM

Tourism is a mainstay of the Egyptian economy. Some estimates suggest that one in seven working Egyptians are somehow involved in the tourist industry. Current estimates suggest that direct and indirect employment in the tourist sector exceed 1,000,000 workers. Egypt possesses a tremendous cultural heritage drawing tourists from all over the world to see its Pharaonic, Roman, Greek, Coptic, and Islamic monuments. The total number of tourists in 1995/96 climbed to around 3.1 million with some 20.5 million tourist nights, up considerably from the previous year. Revenues from the tourism sector reached approximately 11 billion Egyptian pounds or US$200 million in 1995/96, growing some 27% over the previous year. Egypt is also seeking to expand its tourism sector by developing additional types of tourist attractions, such as those for the arts, sports, and adventure. To improve competitive capabilities in the international tourism market, Egypt is upgrading tourist facilities and elements throughout the country.

When you are in Egypt, it is impossible to avoid or ignore the role tourism plays in the economy. Tourism and its effects are seemingly everywhere. Although only 263,600 workers are estimated to work directly in tourism, the downstream effects are felt throughout the population, with the possible exception of small, traditional farmers. From hawkers to tourist buses to taxi drivers to bank clerks, almost everyone seems to be affected by the hordes of foreigners visiting Egypt each year. Tourism slackened substantially in the early 1990s due to adverse reactions to terrorist activity, but this pattern reversed beginning in 1995.

Five-star cruise ships dot the Nile waiting for their passengers. Tourism is a cornerstone of the Egyptian economy.

On 17 November 1997 local criminals carried out the most serious and horrendous terrorist attack against tourists ever perpetrated in Egypt. This event occurred on the west bank of the Nile across from Luxor at the site of Queen Hatshepsut's tomb. Six gunmen dressed in police uniforms rampaged through the ancient site brandishing automatic rifles, hand grenades, and knives. The semiofficial newspaper, *Al Ahram*, reported that 42 Swiss nationals, 10 Japanese, 4 Britons, and 4 unidentified foreigners were killed along with several Egyptians. Among the Egyptians killed were the gunmen who perpetrated the crime. For more information see the section on Terrorism below.

CRIME AND VIOLENCE

Violence and violent crimes in Egypt are extremely rare. When they do occur, they tend to be family related or between individuals who know each other. Rape and attempted rape are virtually unknown since punishment for these crimes is extremely severe, including the death penalty in some cases. Women, even unescorted women, are generally safe on the streets of Egypt. When women are alone on the street it is extremely important to follow local custom regarding dress and appropriate behavior in order to avoid either sexual harassment or verbal abuse.

Sometimes Egyptians seem to be in a heated argument right in each other's face. Frequently, well-wishing passers-by get involved in the dispute and before you know it there will be a whole crowd of people shouting, yelling, and waving their arms. This kind of confrontation can be disconcerting and often scares the uninitiated expatriate because it is easy to misinterpret. In fact, it is fairly common just about anywhere in Egypt and is simply a traditional way of communicating that almost never leads to violence. The best thing to do is to just ignore it and go on about your business. If, for some reason, you happen to be the center of one of these discussions, just stand aside and let them settle it. This could happen if, for example, you asked for directions and two people disagree on what you should do. Another situation where I see this potential is if someone thinks you are being mistreated, cheated, or otherwise treated disrespectfully and feel it is their responsibility to take your side.

Pickpocketing, purse snatching, and petty theft are not uncommon, though they tend to occur most frequently around tourist areas. Obvious precautions certainly reduce or eliminate the risk of petty robbery. One thing that again happens infrequently, but which you must be aware of, is unapproved charges to credit cards. Again, this occurs only rarely and certainly not in the better shops in Egypt.

TERRORISM

Terrorism is a difficult topic to explain not only because it is seemingly random in nature, but also because when acts occur, the number of casualties is typically higher than individual acts of violence. Besides, the very word "terrorist" is enough to scare anyone! One never knows when or where a terrorist will strike or who will be affected. The Penal Code defines terrorism to include the acts of "spreading panic" and "obstructing the work of authorities."

The Egyptian government's anti-terrorist campaign is taking very strong measures to reduce risks of random terrorist violence. Under provisions of the Emergency Law (in effect since 1981), the police may obtain an arrest warrant from the Ministry of the Interior upon showing that an individual poses a danger to security and public order. This act thus nullifies the constitutional requirement of showing that an individual has likely committed a specific crime. During 1996, security forces and police arrested at least 120 members of the Muslim Brotherhood as well as 200 members of a new group, called the Qutbiyoun, which is an offshoot of the Brotherhood. Charges ranged from distributing illegal leaflets, to membership in an illegal organization and inciting the masses against the government.

The Muslim Brotherhood is a political and religious organization founded in Egypt in 1928. Generally anti-Western, it advocates a society based on Islamic principles of social justice as opposed to secular nationalism. Since the 1950s, the Brotherhood and many of its radical offshoots received funding from Saudi Arabia. Initially, this was due to their anti-Communist stance; later it was due to a need to counterbalance Iranian-backed Shiite radicals and the Palestine Liberation Organization and its offshoots. The Islamic Group *(Al-Gamaa'a al-Islamiyya)* broke from the Brotherhood in the mid-1970s. Al-Gamaa'a al-Islamiyya is the group responsible for the attack that killed 18 Greek tourists in Cairo (April 1996), which was until November 1997 the largest casualty count from a single incident in Egypt's modern history. Terrorist groups killed 132 persons in 1996, compared with 200 the previous year. Persons killed included 48 security or police officers as well as 84 civilians. Most attacks were against either authorities or Coptic Christians in Minya, Assiut, Sohag, or Qena. Groups also attacked churches and other properties owned by Christians. These attacks are partially the result of a feud between authorities and families located in these areas stemming from their goal to establish an Islamic state and the perceived economic repercussions of a secular government.

Ten people were killed and numerous wounded on 18 September 1997 when three or more individuals tossed Molatov cocktails under a tourist bus outside the National Museum at Midan Tahrir in Cairo. At the time of this writing the two brothers and principal criminals responsible for this action are in jail awaiting execution. One of the brothers had been recently released from Egypt's main mental hospital where he had been placed following an earlier attack on a major hotel that refused to give him a job. Therefore, this action appears to be separate from any organized anti-government groups that have previously sought to undermine the government of President Hosni Mubarak. Indeed, no known anti-government group has claimed responsibility for the event or association with these criminals.

A new round of attacks began in a little publicized event in Minya in October 1997. At this time, criminals dressed in police uniforms set up roadblocks and killed nine Egyptians, including four off-duty policemen. Since most recent terrorist events have occurred in this region of Egypt, perhaps little thought was given to expansion of this mode of attack to other areas. For whatever reason, security (which was historically less intense in and around the major tourist sites from Luxor south to Aswan) proved to be insufficient when six men attacked tourists on Luxor's west bank on 17 November 1997, killing 64 people. The six perpetrators dressed in police uniforms, believed to be members of Al-Gamaa'a al-Islamiyya, were killed during the subsequent gun battle between the terrorists and police forces. On 18 November, a rival militant group, *Talaa Al Fath*, headed by Ayman Al Zawahari living in Switzerland, reportedly issued a statement to an international news agency warning tourists to stay out of Egypt. According to Richard Engel writing in the *Middle East Times*, the statement said, "Today's military operation in Luxor won't be the last one. Foreigners per se are not targets, but we have warned them about giving money to the Egyptian regime."

Egyptian government officials responded immediately with massive police support in and around all tourist sites in Egypt. Changes were made at the ministerial level when a new Minister of Interior was appointed following the immediate resignation of his predecessor. New plans are under development to reevaluate and refine security measures at all of Egypt's tourist sites. Tourist groups are sure to find their movement restricted, at least in the near future, as forces seek to secure their safety through initial increases in security forces.

International governments also reacted immediately to events in Luxor, which occurred at the beginning of the high tourist season in Egypt. Many governments issued travel advisories and one began special flights to evacuate citizens on the ground in Egypt. Early indications suggest that Egypt's anticipated greatest tourist year ever will fall far short of expectations as a result of many tour group cancellations. Other current events occurring in the Middle East region also will potentially affect travel to the region. I am referring specifically to events in the Arabian or Persian Gulf region which show signs of continuing for some time before being completely settled.

All in all, the number of terrorist incidents declined in recent years making travel throughout Egypt safer during that period than in the previous few years. Nevertheless, recent events indicate a new potential for security concerns. Clearly, tourist movement into certain areas of the country (specifically, Middle Egypt) still requires extra caution. If you plan to travel to this area, it is prudent to seek advice from your local embassy, licensed tour operators, and/or tourist police authorities responsible for the area. Following events in Luxor, standard security measures for tourist groups at all tourist sites have been substantially increased and will likely remain so in the foreseeable future. As always, check for government warnings and advisories to determine relative risks before travelling to the area. Any number of factors not directly related to events in Egypt can make travel to the area unadvisable. As a side note, I would feel remiss if I did not point out that travel within Egypt, even given the most recent drastic events, presents less hazard based on statistical probability of experiencing a violent event, than living in most major U.S. cities. This is not said to diminish the importance and horror associated with the attack in Luxor. It is only presented as a reminder to look at real events and occurrences rather than responding emotionally to the unknown. As in any potentially risky situation, keep your antennae tuned, constantly monitor the situation, and maintain situational awareness to give yourself a greater probability of a safe journey.

– *Chapter Two* –

ANCIENT AND RECENT PAST

A minimal understanding of Egypt's ancient and recent past is useful to the foreign resident for several reasons. First, the major issues affecting contemporary Egyptians, and thus anyone living in the country, have roots in her history. Second, it is impossible to go down any street in Egypt without some kind of recognition of her ancient glory as one of the five centers in the world where civilization developed. Third, ancient Egypt's monuments, temples, mosques, monasteries, and pyramids provide the basis for a substantial portion of her current economy. For a short summary of Middle Eastern dynamics and history, see the work by Spencer listed at the end of this book, which served as the source of much of the recent historical information included in this chapter.

The accomplishments of the ancients defy description. Words like "awe-inspiring" or "incredible" or "spectacular" cannot come close to describing the emotions running rampant through anyone confronted with their first view of the great Hypostyle Hall of Karnak or the Great Pyramid of Khufu. No matter how hard you try to snap a photo that shows what you see, that feeling of being small and inconsequential eludes the camera's eye. Underlying the sheer majesty of Egypt's megalithic monuments is the inevitable acknowledgement of the powerful political mechanism that must surely have been in place to organize such gargantuan projects. You cannot view monuments like the Pyramids, the Valley of the Kings, or the Temple of Karnak without humility and without recognizing Egypt's contribution to the development of all human society.

That being said, I do not intend to write a description of monuments nor an in-depth diatribe on Egypt's history. Instead, I will highlight only the main eras recognized in Egyptian history. If you are interested in a comprehensive treatment of Egyptian history or prehistory, start with the works listed at the end of this book and work your way forward through the myriad of tomes on the subject.

PREDYNASTIC AND DYNASTIC HISTORY

People were living throughout the Nile valley for several thousand years before Egypt as we know it became a unified state. This is generally termed the prehistoric, archaic, and Predynastic periods of Egyptian history. The Predynastic period lasted from about 3150 to 3050 BC. By around 3150 BC, highly stratified states existed in the two separate kingdoms of Upper and Lower Egypt. The boundaries were pretty much as recognized today. Upper Egypt constituted the area from the beginning of the Delta southward, whereas Lower Egypt covered the Delta region. Just as settled village life was inextricably tied to the narrow, elongated fertile strip along the Nile, the river also provided the avenue for traffic and communication.

Most of Egypt's outstanding monuments were constructed during her Pharaonic period. Egyptian dynastic history reckons that Egypt became a unified kingdom at about 3150 BC when King Menes (Narmer) succeeded in unifying Upper and Lower Egypt. There is no historical record of King Menes who placed his capital at Memphis about 25 miles south of current day Cairo. Some think the unification credited to Menes may be more a symbolic than a political act. However, Egypt's initial unification appears to have lasted through the end of the Old Kingdom (ca 2575 – 2150 BC).

In any event, the unity of Egypt seems to have been shattered during the First Intermediate Period (ca 2150 – 2040 BC) which lasted about 100 years. During this time, the central power of the king broke down. Though nominally in service to the pharaoh, nomarchs (rulers of individual nomes or divisions of Egypt) operated virtually independently from central rule.

The anarchy of the First Intermediate Period was followed by a period of restored order under the Pharaoh Mentuhotep I or II (some controversy as to which one). This period was called the Middle Kingdom (ca. 2040 – 1783 BC). Mentuhotep consolidated the administrative power of Egypt at Thebes (modern Luxor). Although the seat of political power shifted on several occasions throughout Egyptian history, from the Middle Kingdom onwards, religious influence emanated from Thebes. The pharaohs of the Middle Kingdom were able once again to institute major architectural projects, which had lapsed during the First Intermediate Period. By the last 50 years of the Middle Kingdom, once again central authority gradually waned.

The Second Intermediate Period lasted nearly 200 years (ca 1783 – 1550 BC). Somewhere around 1663 BC, Egypt was invaded by a group of somewhat mysterious people known as the "Hyksos." The term Hyksos comes from the Greek meaning "rulers over foreign lands." It is not totally clear exactly who the Hyksos were, but they were apparently of Asiatic origin, perhaps from Turkey. Some activities of the Hyksos are very confusing. Even though they continued to tolerate legitimate Egyptian kings, they apparently desecrated monuments and reduced major landowners to poverty. However, importantly, the Hyksos introduced several new technological innovations. Paramount among these was the horse and chariot, which subsequently became a formidable weapon for Egyptian warriors.

If you like historical fiction or dramatizations of this period, check out Wilbur Smith's book entitled *River God* and the sequel, *The Seventh Scroll.* Great reading, but not necessarily totally in line with history! John Anthony West (source for most of the chronology in this chapter) also suggests a series of novels by Joan Grant, the best being *Horus of the Horizon.*

The Hyksos were eventually forced out of Egypt around 1550 BC, which commences the period termed the New Kingdom. The New Kingdom lasted some 500 years during which time Egyptian dominance reigned throughout the region. In popular terms, the New Kingdom is synonymous with the Egypt described in the Old Testament. New Kingdom pharaohs abandoned pyramid building in favor of massive tombs carved into the sandstone cliffs of the Nile's west bank. It is also during this period that the great temples of Thebes were built – Luxor, Karnak, Deir el-Bahari, Medinet Habu, and the Ramesseum.

Egypt's most enduring icon – the Great Pyramids – a legacy of the Pharaonic era.

Until the invasion of the Hyksos, Egypt had been spared large-scale foreign invasion. After that time, Egypt became part of the overwhelming wave of aggressors throughout the Middle East. Under Tuthmosis I (1504 – 1492 BC), Egypt became an imperial power, pushing her borders far into Nubia in the south and to the Euphrates in the northeast. By the time of Ramses II (1300 – 1233 BC), Egypt's monarchs extended their power over much of the Middle East.

Except for the Roman Empire (governed from outside the Middle East), major empires of the region centered successively from four focal points: Mesopotamia (current day Iraq), Asia Minor (Turkey), the Nile Valley (Egypt), and Persia (Iran). Each of these areas served as a power focus two or three times over the ages. Interestingly, at one time or another each major power locus has controlled much or most of the rest of the region, thus providing many of the historical cultural links seen today.

By the beginning of the Third Intermediate Period (ca 1070 - 712 BC), Egypt no longer dominated the Mediterranean but instead retreated to her natural geographic boundaries. During this period, technological advances in the aggressive civilizations throughout Mesopotamia did not spread to Egypt. Consequently, Egypt was unable to wage war successfully against these powers. Once again, relative anarchy ensued, providing the milieu for Libyan mercenaries, who assimilated into Egyptian society during the New Kingdom, to assume powerful positions. Prior to the Third Intermediate Period, much of Egyptian history is reconstructed from archaeological and artistic reconstruction. From this period forward, however, documents remain that provide a much more traditional historical record.

Finally, Egypt began what is termed the Late Kingdom (ca 712 – 332 BC), a period of reunification established under rule of the Nubian pharaoh, King Shebaka. Twice during the Late Kingdom, Egypt came under Persian rule. The Second Persian Invasion succeeded in 343 BC, but lasted only a short time before Egypt came under the rule of the great Macedonian warrior, Alexander the Great.

The Second Persian Invasion marks an important point in Egyptian history. It signifies the beginning of 2,600 years of foreign domination. Independent rule was not reinstated in Egypt until Gamal Abdel Nasser's expulsion of the British puppet, King Farouk, in 1952.

GRECO-ROMAN PERIOD (332 BC – AD 395)

Alexander marched unopposed into Egypt in 332 BC. At the mouth of the Delta, Alexander founded the City of Alexandria designed to be the capital of his empire. For the next nine hundred years, Alexandria was the great center of learning in the Middle East.

When Alexander died in 323 BC, he was succeeded by his able general, Ptolemy, under the nominal rule of Alexander's brother Philip. Once Philip died, Ptolemy became sole ruler, establishing a dynasty that lasted until the death of Cleopatra VII in 30 BC. Alexander's immense empire barely survived his death. His generals carved up the empire and fought among themselves to try to conquer more territory. Ptolemy embraced the Egyptian religion, a practice followed by his successors. Whether for political reasons or sincere belief, the practice helped secure the lands of Egypt under Ptolemaic rule.

The Ptolemies ruled from Alexandria, but became increasingly out of touch with the Egyptian people. In fact, until the last Cleopatra, the Ptolemies did not even speak the Egyptian language. It is during this period that Egypt undertook the last of its grand architectural and sacred artistic development. Temples built in this era have Greek-influenced reliefs as seen, for example, in Edfu, Esna, and Philae.

The Ptolemaic era saw Egypt fully integrated into the affairs of the Near and Middle East. Unlike earlier periods, technological, agricultural, and trade innovations became assimilated into Egyptian life. Egypt still, however, resisted Greek philosophy and religion. Essentially, the Ptolemies kept Egypt independent from other outside rulers. But it was the death of the most famous, and perhaps cleverest, Ptolemaic Queen Cleopatra VII (69 BC – 30 BC), that marked the demise of Egypt's independence once and for all.

Octavian (later Augustus) defeated Cleopatra's military forces under the command of Marc Antony at Actium in 31 BC. Unable to seduce Augustus and thus maintain power over the throne of Egypt, Cleopatra VII committed suicide by clasping the infamous asp to her breast in 30 BC. If you are interested in reading the earliest accounts of Cleopatra VII, see Plutarch's *Parallel Lives*, originally written in the first century.

Under Roman rule, Egypt had little or no political autonomy. Rome used Egypt as its bread basket. Even though Rome ruled Egypt with a tight grip, it was largely tolerant of Egyptian religion. Christianity finally dealt the death blow of Egypt's ancient religion, beginning when Constantine declared it to be the official religion of the empire in AD 333. As can be expected, the new religion took its fastest and firmest hold in the north, where Alexandria became a center of Christianity. It took some two hundred years before the last of the Isis cult died on the island of Philae.

The Egyptian Coptic Church was one of the earliest organized Christian Churches in the world. Today's Copts are considered to be direct descendants of the ancient Egyptians. When Arab invaders in the seventh century brought Islam to Egypt, they were welcomed by the Copts living there. In return, Arab Islamic leaders did not require conversion to Islam. Instead, they protected the Copts, respecting their Christian heritage. Many Copts did eventually convert. They remain the principal minority in Egypt today. Until very recently, Egypt also had a small but established Jewish community. They were treated with similar respect under Islamic rule. However, most of Egypt's Jewish community emigrated to Israel after its establishment as an independent state in 1948.

RECENT HISTORY

Following the Islamic armies, numerous nomadic Arabs settled in the Nile Valley. Egypt came under the rule of the Muslim caliphs ("successors" of the Prophet Mohammed) until the tenth century. At this time, a Shia group broke away, forming a separate government. This group established a new capital, al-Qahirah, in the desert south of Alexandria. During the sixteenth century, Egypt came under the control of the Ottoman Empire, then under the rule of the Mamluks. Originally slaves or prisoners, the Mamluks eventually were freed, subsequently forming a military aristocracy. The Ottomans essentially ceded control of Egypt to the Mamluks, requiring only periodic tribute and taxes from the citizens.

It is during the eighteenth century that Egypt became embroiled in European political dynamics. By this time, the French and British challenged each other for control of trade in the Mediterranean and sea routes to India. In 1798, Napoleon Bonaparte invaded Egypt. However, the British joined forces with the Mamluks and successfully drove the French from Egypt. This left the British and Mamluks in a power struggle over Egypt.

The Ottoman sultan appointed Muhammad Ali to the post of governor in Egypt in 1805. In the end, he was the successor to the disputes between the Mamluks and the British. Although Muhammad Ali was not Egyptian (he was Albanian by birth), his great organizational skills and vision for a rich and powerful Egypt provided the impetus for suppressing the Mamluks. Muhammad Ali's successors ruled in theory on behalf of the Ottoman sultan, but in reality functioned as independent rulers (called *khedives* or "viceroys").

The Suez Canal was opened in 1869 during the leadership of Khedive Ismail. Unfortunately, for Egyptians, Ismail over-extended Egypt financially and was forced to sell the Egyptian government's share of the Canal to the British. As a result, British control over Egyptian finances ensued. A popular revolt threatened overthrow of the khedive system in 1882, but was halted when the British intervened. The British then established a de-facto protectorate, but kept the khedive office in place.

As most know, the Ottoman Empire, long in decline, finally collapsed totally with the end of World War I. The British used Egypt as a staging ground against the Ottomans throughout the War, insuring their interests in the Suez Canal were protected. Since Egypt was technically still part of the Ottoman Empire, Britain officially declared its intention to "defend" the country. Following the end of World War I, a nationalist movement took form in Egypt. Egyptian nationalist leaders formed the *Wafd* ("delegation"), which presented demands to the British. They wanted complete independence for Egypt. When the British refused their demands, the Wafd turned to violence, organizing boycotts, strikes, and terrorist attacks against the British.

Under pressure, the British formally dissolved the protectorate in 1922, but retained certain controls over Egyptians through regulation of foreign policy, defense, and communications. Thus, Egypt's "independence" was a thin shell. Through this process, Egyptians did regain control over their internal affairs. A new constitutional monarchy was established under King Fuad. Neither King Fuad nor his son successor, King Farouk, trusted Wafd leaders.

During the years of the monarchy, the Egyptian military developed a strong corps of professional officers, most of whom were from lower- and middle-class backgrounds. Among this group of professional officers was Gamal Abdel Nasser, who was already an active anti-British demonstrator by the time he entered the newly formed Egyptian Military Academy. When World War II ensued, the British needed a military staging base in North Africa to ensure their control of the Suez Canal. As a result, the British officially reinstituted Egypt as a protectorate. This action energized Egyptian officers into forming a revolutionary movement.

Following World War II, establishment of the state of Israel in May 1948 resulted in Egypt, along with other Arab countries, embarking on an attempt to destroy the new nation. During this action, the Egyptian army was defeated. Officers were appalled at the evident corruption and ineffectiveness of their own government. Nasser and his compatriots attributed the defeat to their government's failures –

not their own weaknesses. They formed a secret organization, the Free Officers, determined to overthrow the monarchy. Other groups seeking to overthrow the monarch existed but the Free Officers developed the best internal organization and support of the army.

The Free Officers launched their revolution on 23 July 1952. In an essentially bloodless coup, King Farouk abdicated the throne. The coup came only six months after "Black Sunday," the burning of Cairo by mobs protesting the continued presence of British troops in Egypt. By the time the monarchy was officially abolished in 1954, Nasser emerged as the clear leader and became president, prime minister, and head of the RCC.

Nasser established ambitious goals for Egypt: to restore dignity and status to Egypt; to eliminate foreign control; and to establish Egypt as the leader of the Arab world. During Nasser's 18 years at the helm of Egypt, many of his goals were accomplished. Nasser finally succeeded in removing the last vestiges of British rule from Egypt. Valiant efforts failed to unify the Arab world, however. The nadir in Nasser's presidency was the "catastrophe" of the Six-Days War with Israel in June 1967.

Under Nasser, Egypt developed a close alliance with the Soviet Union between 1956 and 1967. The World Bank, under strong pressure from the United States, refused funding of Nasser's most important infrastructural project (construction of the Aswan High Dam) due to Egypt's expressed hostility towards Israel. This action triggered Nasser's turn to the Soviet Union. The Soviet Union agreed to finance the dam, which was completed in 1971.

Even though he had been in poor health for some time, Nasser's death came as a shock to many Egyptians. Following his death in 1970, Anwar el-Sadat, his vice president, was installed as president as per constitutional procedure. Sadat, long thought by many to be Nasser's "yes" man, soon showed his strength.

Very shortly after assuming the presidency, Sadat introduced a "revolution of rectification" which he said was needed to correct the errors of his predecessor. Seeking to ally Egypt more closely with the United States, in 1972 he ordered 15,000 Soviet advisors to leave Egypt. In October 1973, Egyptian forces crossed the Suez Canal and broke through Israeli lines in the occupied Sinai. This attack was coordinated with an attack from Syria on Israel's eastern border. The surprise attack initially pushed the Israelis back, but they later regrouped and subsequently regained most of the territory they had lost. Following that, a stalemate highlighted Arab-Israeli affairs until Sadat took a dramatic chance announcing at a meeting of the Egyptian People's Assembly that he was ready to talk to the Israelis in their own house – the Knesset. And he did so. Sadat's foreign policy successes culminated in the 1979 peace treaty with Israel and, subsequently, the Nobel Peace Prize.

On the home front, Sadat was not as successful. Internally, religious leaders and conservative Muslims objected to many of his practices and policies. The poor resented having to pay more for less. The educated classes were angry about claims that the political system was more open when it was not. Sadat's economic policies also worked against him. In 1974, he announced his new policy for opening the door, bringing to an end Nasser's state-run socialist system. Under this plan, called *Infitah*, the economy should have broadened throughout Egypt. Instead, a few people got richer, while the majority of Egyptians were no better off than before. By 1977, the economy was in such a bad state, that Sadat increased bread prices until riots forced him to cancel the increase.

On 6 October 1981, President Sadat and government leaders reviewed an armed-forces parade in Cairo. Suddenly, one of the trucks stopped, men alighted from the truck and headed for the viewing stand from which Sadat and other dignitaries viewed the parade. In the confusion, it seems that Sadat thought the soldiers were coming over to shake his hand. In any event a hand grenade was lobbed at the viewing stand, but did not explode. A second followed, which again did not explode. Finally, the third grenade exploded. At the same time, the assassins leapt out of the truck, and with automatic guns fired into the viewing stands, killing Sadat.

Vice President Hosni Mubarak succeeded Sadat without incident. Mubarak was given emergency powers and approved death sentences for five of Sadat's killers. Mubarak continued the path started by Sadat, that of opening Egypt's economy and government. He continues progress towards eliminating socialism. Though progress sometimes seems slow to the outsider, his policies are carefully designed to allow step-wise progress without undermining cultural values among the populace. Mubarak, like any leader, has his detractors. Principal among these is the conservative religious element that would like to see Egypt's government become less secular. President Mubarak is now serving his third term as President of Egypt.

– Chapter Three –

PUBLIC EGYPT: SIGHTS, SOUNDS AND SURVIVAL STRATEGIES

In this chapter I have picked out my favorite surprises or cultural shocks that beset most people moving to Egypt. It is an attempt to address the most external aspects of the cultural differences you are likely to encounter. Each shock represents a unique stumbling block to the new resident that may add to the overall confusion of being in a new land.

All of the topics in this chapter pertain to the public side of Egypt. Beliefs, customs, and habits of the Egyptian people are covered separately. Only the exceptional tourist experiences offer many of these surprises first-hand, since most tourists are shepherded by tourism agents. Other parts of public Egypt are visible to even the most casual observer. Anyone staying in Egypt for some time or persons on their own in Egypt meet and overcome these cultural differences starting the moment they arrive. While I am sure I have overlooked someone's most shocking initial cultural encounter, I hope your favorites are included.

FIRST IMPRESSIONS

Most people enter Egypt by air at Cairo International Airport, so I will devote this arrival discussion to that port of entry. You may also enter via ship (through Alexandria or Port Said) or by land (for example, from Israel or Jordan). Wherever and however you enter Egypt, your first challenge will be to go through customs to get your feet on Egyptian soil. You will encounter most of the situations listed below no matter how you arrive.

If you are not accustomed to traveling in the Middle East, you may find it surprising that your plane does not pull into a gateway at the terminal. Instead, it will park and passengers will disembark from a remote spot on the tarmac. Buses will arrive to shuttle passengers to the terminal. From there you will enter a secured area and queue to go through customs. Immediately upon arrival you will be escorted to the customs area where your passport and visa will be examined and stamped.

After clearing customs, you will go to another secured area for baggage claim. Before leaving the baggage claim area, you must go through one other checkpoint prior to admittance to Egypt. At this point, you will be asked about certain items you are bringing into the country. Occasionally bags are searched. Of primary interest as of 1996 are video cameras. Don't worry, it is all right to bring the video camera into the country, but remember you must also leave with the camera. As of 1996/97, video cameras are the only pieces of equipment being noted on your passport, but be sure to register any other equipment with officials if the list changes (you will be notified by officials at the airport regarding items you must claim). Basically, the procedure is as follows. When asked, you claim a particular item (i.e., video camera); there is usually no charge to take it into the country but the serial number of the equipment will be recorded into your passport. Sometimes, for exceptionally long term stays, a deposit is required, which is returned to you upon departure from Egypt. In either event, when you leave Egypt, you must show the noted item to customs officials to ensure you are also leaving the country with the same equipment as you brought into Egypt. If you try to leave without the equipment, substantial delays and fines may be imposed (I was told around US$2,000 for a video camera). The reason given for this procedure is that some items have very high import taxes associated with them. Bringing them into the country and trying to leave without them, subjects you to fines and taxes associated with specified items. Be sure to keep all money-change receipts and the custom Form D or other declaration forms (filled in upon arrival) as you may be required to present them upon departure.

On your way through the airport you will pass several banks or money exchanges. Unlike many other countries, the exchange rate you get at airport banks will be comparable to that elsewhere, so if you need to, exchange money into Egyptian pounds at the airport. If you prefer, you can wait to exchange money at your hotel or a bank near to your lodgings. Most taxi drivers will take foreign money now, as will baggage handlers, because they can easily exchange it into Egyptian pounds. However, you are likely to pay more for the service using foreign currency than you would using Egyptian pounds.

Do not be surprised, when you finally walk out onto the sidewalk, to find numerous men running towards you and grabbing your bags. This is your first experience with what is fondly termed running the gauntlet. Sometimes two or more people will seemingly fight over which one carries which bag, all the time yelling at one another in a language which you don't understand (unless you came to Egypt well prepared with a knowledge of Arabic). Each will try to take you to a special taxi driver that will undoubtedly give you the "best price, no problem." The important thing to remember is to negotiate the price before you get into the taxi and before you let someone store your bags in the taxi. This can be difficult because you are tired, confused, and in the midst of a torrent of people all trying to get your attention and "help" you. It can give you the feeling of being a morsel of food on a hot summer's day with flies circling. Just hold your ground and continue saying *"la',"* the Arabic word for "no," if you don't want assistance. Be prepared, however, to pay a tip for any service you accept (and sometimes even if you don't want help, they will just pick up your bags and run – and will still expect a tip). This is where having small Egyptian notes can come in handy. The going rate is about 50 piastres per bag or the equivalent of US$0.15. Do not tip in foreign coins. Should you need additional assistance, you can summon a tourist policeman in an emergency (you should also tip the policeman if he gives assistance).

At some point following your arrival (whether by air, sea, or land), you will begin to notice many men in uniforms, frequently with assault weapons. You will see uniformed guards everywhere in Egypt – on the streets, at all monuments, frequently at hotel entrances – basically everywhere. Some are police, some are tourist police, some represent various branches of the armed services, and some are special forces. There is a standard joke in Egypt, which says that most of the people you see with assault weapons do not have bullets or if they do, the bullets don't fit the gun. I have never trusted this witticism, especially since it would be totally impossible to tell which is which even if it is true. Your best bet is to assume that if there is a gun, the holder has ammunition that fits.

If you are coming from a country where the presence of armed guards on every street is uncommon, the sight of so many guns will probably be a little unsettling until you get used to it. Also, if you are accustomed to going wherever you like in some buildings (including the airport), you will quickly find that entry into many areas is restricted and armed guards are there to ensure security.

Occasionally you will find traffic is at a total standstill because an important dignitary is going somewhere. Troops line the streets in riot gear in these situations. Occasionally armored personnel carriers with troops wearing riot gear sit at strategic locations. Their presence depends on several circumstances, for example, where you are in Egypt or special circumstances of which you may not be aware. New

47

residents and visitors may be particularly alarmed to see an armored personnel carrier outside their hotel. The word on the street is that "they are there for your protection." Frankly, sometimes it seems for show. In Alexandria, for example, the tourist police seem to have less to do than in other cities, and always make a big show. Other times, extra protection is there because of a potential threat of which you are not aware, and they truly are there as a deterrent and for protection.

GETTING ABOUT

Buses

Cairo buses used to scare me to death. Just the thought of trying to get on one seemed an impossible task, and the thought of getting on and never being able to get off flashed through my mind. Fact is, public buses in Egypt can be great fun and economical, but very uncomfortable and time-consuming. Local buses in Alexandria are much less troublesome and easier to use than those in Cairo. By the way, in Egypt driving is on the right side of the street, American style, so bus stops will be on the right as well.

Buses are definitely an economical way to get about, costing about 25-50 piastres for most rides. Buses and minibuses have numbers prominently displayed, usually in the front window and/or on the side of the bus. Unfortunately (if you are new to Egypt), many are printed only in Arabic numbers, but some also display English numbers. Unless you are getting on a bus at one of the main stations, you need to be able to read the numbers quickly because the buses may not come to a complete stop, but only slow down. Sometimes the buses are full when they pull into a station, and even fuller when they pull out the other side a few seconds later. You enter through the back door. Don't wait for people to queue or offer to let you go in front – they probably won't. You just have to push and shove your way onto the bus. You leave the bus through the front door, so if you aren't going far, better start squeezing your way forward as soon as you get on. At some point during your journey, a man will manage to find you to sell you a ticket, so have correct change handy. Buses are great places for pickpockets and the occasional pinch, with all those people squashed together. Therefore, take particular caution with your wallets, purses, and money pouches.

There is a pamphlet sold at newsstands that lists all bus routes for Cairo's buses and minibuses. Unfortunately, it is only in Arabic, so may not be of much help. You will need to know what number bus or minibus will get you to your destination. Sometimes people are helpful, sometimes they are not. If the bus is stationary, the easiest way to find out where a bus is going is to simply yell your proposed destination. The driver (or passengers) will either wave you on or off to another bus. Another strategy, if you don't speak Arabic, is to have someone you know write your destination in Arabic on a small slip of paper. (By the way, this also works well with taxi drivers.) You can then hand the paper to the driver who will tell you if you have the right

A rare sight – an uncrowded bus pulls into the bus station.

bus. Unfortunately, this only works with stationary buses. You probably want to make your first trip during off-peak hours when buses are a little less crowded.

Cairo's main local bus and minibus terminal is in front of the Nile Hilton at Tahrir Square (Midan Tahrir). Minibuses are definitely a little easier than regular buses. Supposedly, rules limit the number of passengers on minibuses, and people are not allowed to crowd each other or stand. Like many rules in Cairo transportation, I have yet to see one where every inch of standing space wasn't taken, often with extra people hanging on the side steps of open buses.

Several other types of buses operate in Egypt. In smaller towns and villages, as well as in Cairo, private micro-buses (vans or trucks) meander through the streets. They do not have signs, so it is difficult to tell exactly where they are going or if they follow a specific route. If you think you want to get on one, yell out your destination as it passes. If the driver is going there, he will stop for you.

Everywhere you look, you will see tour buses prominently marked. These are private buses run by agencies, which operate package tours with stops at places of archaeological interest. Many tourist (excursion) buses offer excellent services from Cairo to major destinations throughout Egypt. Intra-City buses provide an easy way to get from one major city to another, particularly from Cairo north and eastwards, to Alexandria, Port Said, Ismailia, and Suez. First class buses and jet buses have limited seats, usually 40. Your ticket will give you an assigned seat for these buses. These buses are air-conditioned and quite comfortable. Some provide in route snack service and videos.

Trains
The Egyptian railway system covers over 7,000 kilometers (4,350 miles). Principal routes connect Cairo with Aswan, Port Said, the Suez, and Alexandria. There are three classes of service offered. Third class is Spartan and rather uncomfortable. Second class is most useful for short distances. Neither third nor second class is air-conditioned.

First class trains provide air-conditioning, meal service or dining cars, and sleeping compartments for major routes. Refreshment services customarily offer sandwiches, sweets, pastries, coffee, tea and other beverages. Reservations may be made at the Midan Ramses Station in Cairo (telephone, 753555), the Central Station in Alexandria, or through any travel agency. Be sure to make reservations in advance, not only for sleeping berths, but also for seats on regular trips. Unless there is a breakdown, Egyptian trains operate on schedule.

Taxis

Taxis are everywhere. To get one, keep your eyes peeled for an empty one and simply wave your arm. In some cases, even a taxi with a fare will stop and you can share the taxi. There are two theories on figuring out how much a taxi should cost. When you are new to the area, negotiate the fare for your trip before you enter the taxi. Once you enter the taxi, they have you and the rate will surely be higher. Some taxis have meters, but they rarely work, so you are on your own to get a good rate. Plan on being ripped-off until you get the feel for looking like you know what you are doing. Things you can count on: (1) taxi fares are higher around tourist areas; (2) as a foreigner, taxi drivers will always try to charge you more than an Egyptian for the same service, no matter how good a negotiator you are.

Still, taxi rates are reasonable and one of the most convenient ways to get around in Egypt. Once you begin to know your way around your favorite places, you will even be able to tell the driver the easiest way to get where you want to go. You will also know reasonable fares and be able to state the price you are willing to pay up front, eliminating the bargaining. Until then, be prepared for drivers pretending they do not know how to get where you want to go (even major landmarks) and taking you for long drives throughout the city. Should you come across one of the few totally unscrupulous taxi drivers that refuses to take you where you want to go without unscheduled stops at an uncle's or brother's or sister's shop, simply refuse to get out of the taxi

when he stops. If he says he won't go further unless you get out, get out and walk off yelling to try to get attention from a nearby policeman or shop owner. In most cases, someone will come out and take your side. Egyptians do not like cheats either. If this doesn't work, take the taxi driver's number (listed on a plaque or paper in the taxi) and report him to the authorities.

The second strategy is to not negotiate the fare. An appropriate rate for going across Cairo (perhaps 30 minutes ride) is about E£3. Once you look like you know what you are doing, you will be better able to get away with this strategy. Longer journeys will still need to be negotiated. For example, from central Cairo, it will cost you E£15–20 to go to the airport or E£10 for a trip to the pyramids. Again, if you are clearly a tourist or novice expatriate, count on the driver trying to charge you more.

A strategy I learned from a long-term expatriate to ensure drivers don't demand more than the negotiated fare is to always carry a large quantity of very small Egyptian bills – 25 and 50 piastre notes are best. When you get to where you are going, do not pay the driver while you are sitting in the taxi. Get out of the taxi, making sure to take all of your belongings with you. Then hand the driver a wad (not neatly folded stack) of small denomination notes through the front window. Taxis are not air-conditioned, so the windows are always down and provide an excellent way to pay the driver. Then walk away. Unless you have tried to cheat the driver, by the time he has counted the money, you will be well on your way. Never try to cheat a taxi driver. They can and do yell loudly, attracting the attention of numerous police standing around with nothing better to do than settle the dispute. Even if you do not have piastre notes, small bills are always better than large ones. Some drivers may not have exact change, or at least say they don't have exact change.

By the way, a word of warning for women riding in taxis: do not ride in the front seat or next to the driver unless you are willing to run the risk of the driver's hands wandering a little. While they would never consider such affronts to an Egyptian or Muslim woman, foreign women are fair game. One reason for this is that no Muslim or Egyptian woman would place herself in the position of being accessible to such confrontations; therefore (according to their logic), if a woman places herself next to a man, it must be for a reason, so it is all right to touch her.

The Metro

The Metro in Cairo is exceptionally good if you happen to be going somewhere on its limited route. It provides the fastest and easiest way to get around Cairo if you are going near to the places it connects. The Metro system is extremely modern, air-conditioned, and clean throughout. The first car (two cars during peak hours) on each train are reserved for women only. You will occasionally see women in other cars, but women definitely prefer the women's cars.

Station names can be confusing, so be sure to know the station name that takes you near to where you want to go. The Metro line runs from Helwan northeast to El Marq station. It has 22 stops, but only the five stations in central Cairo are underground. Finding stations is easy. Look for the signs with a big red M in a blue star. The underground stations usually have several exits, so you need to know which one takes you where you are going above ground. If you go out the wrong one, you can end up a block or more from where you intended.

There is also a line under construction linking the Mubarak Metro Station (located at Ramses Station) to Shobra. Several extensions and new lines are planned for the Metro, so be sure to check which are open and operational when you get there. For example, an extension of the Helwan-El Marq line is scheduled to connect directly to the airport. Another extension is planned for connecting Mubarak Station to Gezira and Dokki, which will extend to the Giza suburbs. Still another line will eventually connect Embaba to Salah Salam.

About halfway down the steps to the Metro stations or outside the gates of the Metro station, posted signs indicate these are non-smoking areas. Believe the signs! If you do not, you are likely to have police pull you aside and issue a ticket on the spot that can be both expensive and time-consuming by the time you get it paid.

Traffic

Hang on to your hat, now you get to experience Egyptian traffic Cairo style! Traffic in Cairo is notoriously horrible! Most people tell you there is no logic to driving in Egypt. Egyptian traffic does not defy explanation, but it does take some understanding.

Cairo driving is extremely aggressive. The first rule is, if there is room for your car, take it. If there is not and you can bluff someone else, go for it. I have been in small buses whose driver bluffed out larger buses by sheer guts. Other drivers have bumped vehicles to get a space first. I have even had drivers pull bumpers off parked vehicles because "they were parked too close to the corner (to make a turn) and should have known better."

If you arrive at night, you may get a special treat. People drive with their lights off at night going as fast as room allows. Several explanations have been given for driving at night without lights such as: "I don't want to bother the driver in front of me." Others think keeping lights on bothers oncoming traffic or runs the battery down.

Another thrill is heading into oncoming traffic when you least expect it. If you are on a road and there is room in oncoming traffic, your driver may dart into oncoming traffic "lanes." I say "lanes" because some major streets are actually divided. However, traffic lane markers and stripes are not painted on many roads. When lane markers are painted, it is usually on major highways or thoroughfares. Even on highways, lane markers are frequently ignored. There appears to be no such thing as a "no-passing" zone.

Just to give you a feel for some of the situations you may encounter, I will relate a few of my own experiences. I have had drivers who when out on a highway and seeing nothing, went into the oncoming lanes because the road was better. Also, my drivers have decided to go up crowded one-way streets the opposite direction to the traffic to shorten the journey. By the way, these are fairly normal occurrences and considered to be no problem. Little bumps between cars are frequent and many of the vehicles you see all over Egypt have numerous dents. Since traffic is slow much of the time, small bumps rarely cause any injury. A basic tip is to expect anything – you will probably experience it sometime during your stay. If you are squeamish, definitely do not ride in the front seat of a bus or car.

Unless you are accustomed to extremely aggressive driving (neither the Los Angeles Freeway nor Houston traffic constitutes extremely aggressive driving), do not plan to drive in Cairo. Until you get accustomed to driving habits, it is probably best for you to use local taxis, buses or the Metro.

The principal branches of Egypt's highway network are Cairo to Alexandria (desert and Delta routes); Cairo to Port Said and Ismailia; Cairo to Suez; Cairo to el-Fayum; Cairo to Aswan; and Suez to Hurghada. These routes are kept in good condition. Other main highways are paved, but frequently in need of repair. Remaining

Just find a spot and squeeze in on one of Egypt's crowded streets.

roads are dirt. Desert tracks lead to the secondary oases, but are recommended for only highly skilled drivers with knowledge and experience in desert driving.

Travel permits are not required for motorists using the major routes in Egypt. However, certain roads may be used only if you are in possession of permits. These routes include the secondary roads of the delta, the coastal road to Libya, the track along the Suez Canal between Ismailia and Suez, the Sinai, St. Catherine's Monastery, and some roads leading to the oases, especially those to Siwa and Baharia. Travel permits may be obtained from the Travel Permits Department, located at the corner of Sharia Sheikh Rihan and Sharia Nubar in Cairo.

You should also be aware of the dangers of off-road travel in Egypt. Old mines from previous conflicts remain buried in some areas of the country. Mine fields are not easily recognizable because signs do not mark them. Instead areas containing mines are enclosed by barbed wire, so definitely do not drive into areas enclosed by barbed wire. Another clue that you may be in an area where old mines remain are deserted tank embankments. Also avoid driving through built-up sand on roads. These may hide land mines that have shifted due to flash flooding in desert areas.

Traffic Police

Numerous uniformed traffic police occupy small guardhouses and corners all along the streets of Cairo. Their precise purpose is a bit perplexing. In some of the central tourist areas, traffic police actually do stop cars to allow pedestrians to cross, but don't count on this or you could wait all day to cross the street. Although traffic police are located at most big intersections, they are mostly there for decoration or special circumstances. Except at certain times of the day in certain areas of the city, traffic lights (when they exist) are ignored. Only well versed Egyptian drivers can discern the hand-signals given by traffic police indicating when it is actually time to obey them. Your best bet if you are new to Egyptian driving is to watch what other drivers are doing and follow suit.

As I mentioned, many newcomers are at first overwhelmed by the traffic and see no logic in its pattern. This is especially true with horn honking. You will notice immediately that horns seem to be honking incessantly all day and all night. Horns communicate a driver's intentions to other vehicles and pedestrians alike. As a general rule of thumb, one honk means "I am here and coming" or is used to signal "thanks" after passing a vehicle. Two honks mean "I am passing you." Three honks mean "I am coming on fast – watch out!" It is actually a very efficient way of communicating in a city where lanes, lights, and Western rules of right-of-way are nonexistent. Automobile lights can serve the function of a horn at night, and are used mostly to let other drivers and pedestrians know you are coming. Sometimes lights and horns are used simultaneously.

Motorcycles, Bicycles, Donkeys, and Donkey Carts

Interspersed among the mass of cars zig-zagging and honking are people using various other forms of transportation. Bicycles and motorcycles weave in and out among the cars. They often have either little horns or bells. Sometimes they have neither and you will hear a hissing sound to warn you of their presence.

Donkeys and donkey carts intermingle with car, truck, and bus traffic on overpasses, main streets, and alleys. People riding donkeys meander along through the traffic and are seemingly unaware of the pandemonium around them. Donkey carts are still a popular means of transporting goods throughout Egypt. The turmoil of Cairo traffic provides no exception. Drivers just go around these slower forms of transport. In many cases, donkeys and donkey carts seem to get the right of way, apparently because their movement is less flexible. Except in the central business district of Cairo, you will also frequently see people (children or adults) walking or herding a water buffalo or goats on the roads or highways. They do not stay on the side of the road, but instead take their place on the road or highway along with the faster moving traffic. Camels are rarely seen on the streets of Cairo except around the area of the pyramids or near the camel *souk* (market). Other than for tourist purposes, camels are generally used on the farms to transport heavy agricultural products such as cane.

Motorcycles can be a particular hazard if you are not careful. They tend to go faster than most cars and dart in and out at an alarming speed. I was actually hit by a motorcycle late one evening in an alley near Cairo's old medieval quarter. It happened because I froze when I heard the motorcyclist's incessant horn beeping. Unfortunately, when I heard the horn, I didn't know whether to move left or right or what, so I just stopped, thinking that would give the driver the best opportunity to go wherever he wanted. To my surprise the driver was already committed and screeching to a stop. He didn't quite make it before he reached me. Angry shop owners immediately came out of shops yelling at the motorcycle driver. As far as I can tell, the best approach to avoiding collisions with motorcycles is to keep your ears perked and eyes constantly alert, especially when on smaller streets or alleys.

These traffic patterns hold throughout Egypt, however in smaller cities traffic certainly is not as congested as in Cairo. Traffic in Alexandria is somewhat less troublesome than in Cairo, but faster. Lane markers occur more frequently on Alex's streets, but again are sometimes ignored. Some streets, for example the Corniche, become one-way during certain times of the day in Alexandria. One does not go against traffic in Alexandria.

Even with the abundance of automobile and truck traffic in Cairo, most people seem to be on foot. Egyptians walk everywhere. When going short distances, a mile or two, walking is the most practical means of getting anywhere because it is faster.

Survival on Foot

Absolutely, positively the most important skill you must learn is pedestrian survival. The key words for pedestrian survival are "situational awareness." Egyptian drivers are alert not to hit pedestrians in case they might have a family member who would seek retribution. Do not count on their acuity for your survival! Rural towns are considerably less congested than are the cities, but this only means the drivers are less alert to wayward walkers. Once you learn to cross the streets successfully in Cairo, and maintain your level of situational awareness when being a pedestrian in general, you will have the greatest probability of living in Egypt unscathed by bumps, hits, and slam-dunks. While the same strategies work in all areas of Egypt, don't forget the traffic tends to move faster in Alexandria, so where you might walk in Cairo, you will need to be on a dead run in Alex.

First, slick soled shoes are a hazard. Like streets in most places, Cairo's streets tend to slope downward from the center. They also tend to be covered with a fine layer of the infamous dusty sand. Sand on sloping streets makes for bad traction. You never know when you are going to have to sprint the extra few feet to avoid an oncoming car picking up speed. Unless you want to end up lying under a parked car, or worse yet, the moving vehicle, shoes with soles that allow some kind of traction work best.

Second, don't worry about being at an intersection to cross a street. If you want to go across, head out into the traffic like the rest of the population. As previously mentioned, rarely do you find places where police or lights stop traffic for pedestrians to cross. Even when they do, there is usually someone coming around a corner right into crossing foot traffickers. So how do you get across? Well, the easiest way when you first arrive is to find some Egyptians who want to cross where you do and go with them. You must be careful not to lag behind them, however, because they are probably gauging their steps by not only what is coming in one "lane," but what is coming in several. You may have just enough time to get across one line of cars, and stop as others in the next line speed past, only to quickly dart another lane's worth to stop again. It is frequently a zig-zag process. Whatever you do, don't try carrying on a conversation while crossing the street. This tends to slow people down and diverts their attention from oncoming cars, buses, trucks, bicycles, donkeys, donkey carts, and motorcycles. You not only must keep your eyes peeled for movement from every direction, but you must also keep your ears attuned to the sound of hisses, horns, and bells. Don't forget two-wheeled vehicles tend to dart in and out among the bigger varieties, and may not be visible when you start between two cars. Also, do not wait for cars to stop before crossing the street (they likely never will, although the occasional Cairene may take pity on a foreigner). In really congested areas, slowed or non-moving traffic makes your progress easier.

Third, pedestrian traffic is not limited to sidewalks. Nor is wheeled traffic necessarily limited to streets. People walk anywhere and everywhere there is room to move (just like cars go anywhere there is space, so do people on foot). Bicycles and motorcycles weave through pedestrians whether on the sidewalk or in the streets. They often appear as if by magic out of some little nook or alley between buildings which may be hardly perceptible to the newcomer. Again, keep your eyes and ears open.

Asking Directions

If you ask someone for directions, be prepared to get an answer. Almost all people are willing to try to help you. However, they may not know where you want to go. It is a typical Egyptian trait to always have an answer to a question, whether or not the respondent knows where you want to go. It is simply not considered appropriate for most Egyptians to say, "I don't know." Alternatively, a person may indicate they do not understand what you are asking rather than admit to not knowing what you are look for. More likely they will point you in some direction whether it is the right one or not. The result, of course, is you may find yourself wandering in circles when where you wanted to go was only a short distance from where you began. Arm yourself with an accurate street address if you want to get good directions. Getting to the general area of town and simply asking for a place name results in many a wild goose chase.

SIGHTS, SMELLS, AND SOUNDS

Air Pollution

With massive traffic jams and no quality control on exhaust systems, Cairo air pollution at certain times of the year gives you the feeling of wandering London during a heavy fog – one that smells like exhaust fumes. Cairo's air pollution is the worst in Egypt. Especially in summer, when heat inversions are common and winds from the Nile are least, the air becomes laden with smog. From a distance, Cairo takes on a reddish glow. Smog is distinctly less in winter than in summer. It seems that bringing the Metro or subway system online has reduced the air pollution somewhat, though smog still remains a serious problem in Cairo.

Smoking

The attitude of Egyptians towards smoking is best depicted at a place called the "Piano Bar" in the World Trade Center. The so labeled "non-smoking" area is a chair nailed to the wall at the edge of the ceiling. Egypt is a land of smokers. If you cannot tolerate cigarette smoke, you had best change your ways, take plenty of antihistamines or stay out of Egypt. There are few non-smoking areas anywhere in Egypt and none in restaurants or most public places. A few of the better hotels are now advertising non-smoking rooms. Other than that, the only non-smoking zones are the Metro, some museum areas, the occasional elevator (not all), and a few other special sites.

Smoking etiquette requires anyone who is smoking in a meeting or group to offer everyone else in the group a cigarette. Foreign cigarettes are particularly preferred, so be prepared. If you do not smoke, do not feel compelled to accept a cigarette when offered. Egyptians do not mind if you don't smoke, however, they expect to be able to smoke in your presence in any event. Expect your guests to smoke, whether in a business meeting or when visiting your home. Your personal preference for non-smoking does not count.

Unless there are overriding reasons for not smoking in an area, for example sensitive equipment that might malfunction with too much smoke (such as computers) or explosive chemicals, people smoke. The best efforts of health officials are making only a minimal impact toward stopping or limiting one of the favorite Egyptian pastimes.

Smoking is a man's prerogative in Egypt. Egyptian women who smoke rarely do so in public. Other than cigarette smoking, which is done everywhere, the preferred method is the water pipe. Water pipes are smoked in restaurants, at home, and in the myriad of small street cafes where men congregate, drinking coffee or tea while playing table games. Water pipes are called *shisha* pipes in Egypt; a word derived from the Arabic term meaning hashish. The tobacco smoked in these pipes is not hashish. It is a gummy mixture of molasses and tobacco, sometimes with a flavor added such as apple.

Noise

Many people find the high noise level in Egypt to be quite bothersome. To me, Cairo seems to be much quieter than it used to be. I remember seeing a video once where the person was asking for a "quiet room" at an Egyptian hotel. Laugh and forget it! If you are looking for silence and solitude, I recommend going to the desert alone or another country, although suburbs are much quieter than central Cairo. The only places in central Cairo that are reasonably quiet are some of the interior rooms in the large five-star hotels. Even then, traffic noise may filter through the walls.

What kinds of sounds can you expect? Well, I have already alluded to the traffic sounds – horns, cars, trucks, donkey carts. Even without these urban noises, Egypt is alive with sound. Beginning before sunrise, there are the calls to prayer that echo from the minarets of mosques all over the country five times a day. The first time the 4:30 a.m. call to prayer startles you from a sound sleep, you may shake your head trying to figure out what is happening. After a few days, the calls to prayer promote a peaceful and stabilizing feeling, letting you know that all is right in the world.

Another aspect of Egyptian culture is the seeming need to have music all the time. Every shop and cafe, especially in the tourist areas, has music playing constantly. And it is loud! At first, Egyptian music sounds sharp to the Western ear because it is a quartertone out from Western music. Eventually Egyptian music weaves its magic of romance, often soulfully singing of unrequited love. Lively belly dancing songs incite movement in the most sedate guests.

The noises of Egypt may be disruptive for the first couple of weeks, but in no time it will feel normal. After you have been there for a while, you will only notice when the sounds are out of the ordinary. At this point, silence may become deafening.

Colors of Egypt

Egypt is a country of stark color contrasts. It is almost inconceivable until you have seen it to visualize the drastic contrast between the desert and the "green." The "green" refers to the areas irrigated from the Nile throughout the country. Green areas tend to be a mile or less along either side of the river. Literally, where the irrigation stops the desert begins. The "green" is often very tropically lush with much shade and waving palms. The desert is stark with few immediately visible lifeforms.

Except for small areas along the Nile and parks, Cairo is a palette in monochrome. Buildings made of native stone or concrete match the surrounding desert environment. The basic color of the city is a slightly grayer shade of tan than the desert proper, which tends to be a light golden tan with a very slight reddish hue. In winter, the sky may be bright blue, especially in the mornings. However, even in winter,

There is a sharp contrast between the rich vegetation of the floodplain and the stark environment of the desert.

the afternoon sky fades to a lighter shade of blue. Up and down the Nile, morning winter skies are clouded with smoke from open cooking and heating fires. The smoke settles along the river due to the high population density at the river's edge.

During summer months, the sky tends to be grayish light blue that fades into white. The pale sky against the desert tan increases the stark contrast between green and desert. It also adds to the monochrome effect in cities. Egyptians delight in adding color at every opportunity. Brightly colored household decorations, rugs, and even clothing sparkle against the sandy colored world. The style of furniture most popular in middle and upper class homes is rather baroque with intricately carved heavy pieces of wood. Couches and chairs are frequently covered in decorative brocade fabrics.

Dirt

What commonly passes for dirt in Egypt is really very finely powdered sand. It is everywhere! Sand blows in the air, seeps through doors and windows, and even lodges itself under the finger and toenails. The sand is so finely grained that when you rub it between your fingers, it does not feel particularly harsh. Sand blows in from the desert and cannot be eliminated or controlled, even with the most zealous attempts by Egyptians. Shop keepers and hotel attendants constantly wash sidewalks, foyers, and any other surface on which dust can collect. Floors are almost constantly being swept or washed with soapy water and a 'squeegee-gee,' one of those rubber blades attached to a broom or mop handle used for window cleaning. Sidewalks are frequently hosed down and swept to try to control the dust.

Truly, nothing works for long. The climate is so arid that within minutes the dust dries, starting its cycle of collecting everywhere once again. Most stores, homes, and hotels have one or two bristle mats for wiping your feet when you enter. It is a common courtesy to wipe your feet carefully when entering any establishment or home.

In some cases, when you enter some homes you may even be expected to remove your shoes. I have always heard of this custom, but have never actually seen it practiced. So the best advice is, do not remove your shoes unless everyone else has removed theirs. Do what your host or others guests do. Removing shoes is particularly un-wieldy to Westerners because they usually wear socks or some type of hose to protect their feet from direct contact with their shoes. You will find that, except when dressed in Western business attire (males and females), most Egyptians do not wear hose or socks. The most common shoes are open, sandal type shoes. On the street, especially among the working class, "flip-flops" are the shoes of choice.

Trash and Garbage

Initial perceptions of the streets of Egypt definitely shock the most experienced of travelers. Everything looks dirty. Part of this is due to the monochrome color of Cairo. Another contributing factor is the result of constant building and renovation throughout Egypt. Unused building materials and numerous piles of debris are usually left wherever they fall, whether on streets, sidewalks or roofs. Once left, construction litter tends to stay. Clearing debris away is clearly a low priority. As a result, much of Egypt looks perpetually under construction or as a friend pointed out, "like a war zone."

Garbage collection is a totally different issue. Household garbage is collected regularly. Cairo's "unofficial" refuse collectors, the *Zabbaleen*, collect two-thirds of the garbage. "Official" collectors collect the remaining refuse. The largest Zabbaleen settlement is Manshiet Nasser. Their entrepreneurial expertise has resulted in an intricate social structure surrounding refuse recycling. Here different families specialize in different materials. Families sort through rubbish, dividing it into plastics, metals, paper, rags, bones and organic matter.

Trucks are rapidly replacing the customary donkey pulled carts for transporting garbage through the city. Most flats and villas have back entrances where garbage is collected.

Trash and litter present unique problems for most cities throughout Egypt. People drop trash and litter just about everywhere in Egypt. In fact, finding a trash bin is almost impossible in most cities. Trash collects on the sidewalks and on the edges of streets – anywhere it can find a place to settle. No amount of picking it up by people employed for that purpose controls the trash appearing on the streets daily.

A major exception to the litter problem is the Metro system and some newer areas of the city. Trash bins are strategically placed at Metro stations. Serious fines and a side visit to the local police station can result from failure to use trash bins at the Metro.

Butchers, Street Vendors, and Food Hygiene

Egyptians are by tradition quite concerned with cleanliness. Part of this is due to the teachings in the *Qur'an* (the Islamic Holy Book). This is evident not only in attempts to control nature's sandy penetrations, but in concern with hygiene associated with religious practices. All exposed parts of the body (for example, face, hands and feet) must be washed before entering the mosque for prayer. A lot of outsiders don't know that desert sand is considered to be a cleansing agent under

67

some circumstances. For example, if a Muslim is in the desert and unable to "wash" with water before prayer, he may ritually "wash" with sand.

Concerns for prayer hygiene do not seem to transcend to food preparation habits among many lower- and middle-class Egyptians. Open-air markets predominate. Food is sold, butchered, and prepared amid the street clutter. Street vendors, small walk-up shops for prepared food and drinks, and open-air markets abound throughout Egypt. Animal carcasses hang in the open air without refrigeration. Dinner "on the hoof" stands around waiting to be slaughtered or sold for home preparation. Look on any street and you are likely to see a woman walking with a basket full of live geese or chickens on her head returning from the market to prepare dinner.

If you plan to buy your own meat, it is important to identify a good, reputable butcher whose meats are slaughtered at government butchering facilities to ensure the least likelihood of getting tainted meat. Meat slaughtered at government butcheries will be marked by big red stripes painted on the sides of the carcass. Probably, the best way to find a good butcher is to ask around among your friends or acquaintances that have been in Egypt for some time. They will be in the best position to tell you the safest places to purchase meat and fowl.

As mentioned previously, food prepared by street vendors or in small local cafes is everywhere in Egypt. In many of the smaller cities, these are the only places, except restaurants associated with hotels, to get prepared food. Since many, many eating places in Egypt are open-air or in buildings with doors and windows open, again you may not find the shiny, disinfected cooking surfaces people have come to expect in many parts of the world. Only the bigger cities have chain restaurants or four- and five-star dining facilities.

Better restaurants and hotel kitchens are usually quite clean and sanitary. Great care is taken, especially due to concern for tourists, to maintain safe food handling and preparation in these establishments. If you are particularly nervous about "getting germs," it is probably best to limit your eating out to these types of places, at least at first. Egyptians everywhere pride themselves on hospitality and high quality service. Special care is taken to ensure table settings and foods are attractive, clean, and pleasant to the senses. Courtesy is a given.

Personally, I tend to "eat like an Egyptian." If Egyptians eat the food, I eat the food. But like anyone else, I have particular likes and dislikes, so some types of food I avoid. There are a couple of little tricks that help avoid some of the most common sources of bacteria that can result in diarrhea, or "Pharaoh's curse," as it is referred to by tourists. Most of the time Pharaoh's curse is not serious, just uncomfortable. One neat trick I learned from my Egyptian friends to avoid getting bacteria from salads is to top them with freshly squeezed lemon juice or a little vinegar. Whereas cooking kills bacteria, fresh salad ingredients harbor the little culprits. Anything with a lot of acid will often take care of the squiggly bacteria that can hide on freshly washed lettuce, cucumbers, and tomato skins. One of the greatest street dining delights are *felafel* (fried chickpea) sandwiches. They

One of the many street vendors seen throughout Egypt.

69

are usually served with shredded lettuce and chopped tomatoes on top of the felafel in a piece of Egyptian bread. Just ask the vendor for a piece of lemon and most will gladly accommodate you. I even follow the Egyptian style and squeeze lemon on salads at five-star restaurants or at home – just in case.

Frankly, if you are going to stay in Egypt for any time, you must throw aside some ingrained notions of what constitutes cleanliness about food. Eat only well done meat, fowl, fish, or eggs no matter who cooks them.

Drinking Water

Most guidebooks warn visitors not to drink the local water, eat food on the street, or partake of fruits and vegetables that cannot be peeled and/or cooked. Only you know your own constitution and body's immune system. I would point out that if you are going to be in Egypt for some time and plan to follow Western standards of hygiene, you will have to sequester yourself in a hermetically sealed room (there are none that I know of in Egypt). It is impossible to maintain practices foreign to the land for extended periods of time. Until you can get used to a little dirt and some germs in your system, you will have to follow precautions without a doubt, but I suspect that this cannot continue for long periods of time. Besides, it will not be long before you forget to brush your teeth with bottled water (and you will probably find you do not get a major case of diarrhea doing this).

Most major cities state their tap water is potable. Cleanliness of rural water supplies is considerably more problematic. Usually in small towns and villages, water is drawn from wells or piped in, but cannot be considered potable. Many people get a slight diarrhea when drinking water in rural places. Giardia, one of those bad little parasites which lodges in the intestinal tract, is more likely to be found in rural rather than big city water supplies.

One of the habits I find most interesting among some foreigners revolves around their obsession for ice in drinks. People who religiously carry bottled water so as not to get germs from tap water – the same ones who even brush their teeth with bottled water – turn right around and order ice for their drinks. They never once ask themselves where the water comes from that makes the ice. Ice is made from tap water.

A word of caution: if you are buying bottled water, make sure the seal is not broken when you get the water. There is little concern in big hotels and restaurants. At these places, waiters delight in presenting the chilled water bottle, pointing out the unbroken seal, and ceremoniously breaking the seal for you. On the other hand, some street vendors take old bottles, fill them with tap water, and sell them to customers as bottled water. If someone tries to sell you a bottle of water with the seal broken, politely request another bottle with the seal intact. If they say this is all they have, thank them and go to another vendor.

After a while, you will begin to slack off on the bottled water and "germ-free" imperative. This is particularly true if you are integrating into Egyptian society. When you are invited to someone's home, it is extremely rude to refuse your host's hospitality and not eat their food, whether it is a tomato and cucumber salad or fresh grapes. Usually, you will be offered a variety of drinks such as colas or fruit juice as well as water. If you are still on a strict regimen of bottled water, and water is what you want to drink with your meal, just take your water with you. Everyone understands the newcomer's concern with drinking water. So, it will not seem rude or even unnecessarily strange for you to be cuddling a bottle of water when you appear (unless, of course, you have been living there for six months or a year, in which case you will be perceived to be very strange indeed).

You will not find chilled, public drinking fountains in Egypt, except perhaps in better hotels. Instead, you will notice large pottery jugs full of water located at various fairly inconspicuous places along the streets. The jugs keep the water cool and are there for all to drink. These are public drinking fountains, Egyptian style. You will notice that people walk along, stop, say a few words (perhaps), pour water into the community cup, take a drink of water and continue on their way. Unless you are well adapted to Egyptian life, it is probably best to avoid drinking from public water jugs.

Public Toilets

Go before you leave home! Always take toilet paper or tissues with you – just in case (if you use them). You might also want to carry a plastic, disposable bag for discarding toilet paper in case you have to use a local toilet that doesn't have a place to dispose of it. If you plan to be out all day around town and need facilities, the best bet is to find a friendly restaurant, order something, and use the facilities there. Public toilets are few and far between in most Egyptian cities. They do exist although may be overlooked by the casual observer. In the older parts of the city, entrances to public toilets often look like an entrance to a Metro station (without the prominent signs).

If you have not used a traditional toilet, be prepared for a shock. The typical, traditional toilet is a hole in the ground with two footplates on either side. Usually there is a hose with a handle to turn on the water for cleaning yourself. The hose should be on the left side for easy access by the left hand, the one appropriate to use for these functions. If you prefer toilet paper, bring your own. Women will find tights, leotards, and other clothing that must be totally removed to be a real problem in traditional toilets.

Most modern flats, villas, restaurants, and hotels have facilities with modern flush toilets. Since the system isn't geared to handle large quantities of toilet paper, if you see a bucket on the side, place the paper there. If there is an attendant, it is appropriate to tip the attendant upon departure.

Handicap Facilities

Do not plan to find mobility ramps for the handicapped in Egypt. Some larger tourist hotels have sloped walks useful to wheelchairs;

however, most hotels, restaurants, shops, and flats require people to be able to walk and climb some stairs. Once into buildings, even though many have elevators, some lifts are quite small, designed to hold two or three individuals. Many elevators, especially in older buildings, require the passenger to physically be able to close outside doors and interior gates as well as run the elevators. Older elevators also have a tendency to stop slightly out of line with the floor, thereby making entry/exit hazardous. Access to underground Metro stations requires stair mobility. Visits to most antiquities and tourist sites also require people to be able to climb stairs and walk substantial distances. In general, getting around for mobility handicapped individuals is all but impossible without hired assistance.

Animals

In a society with little mechanized equipment such as Egypt, many animals serve as beasts of burden. Bony looking donkeys carry heavy loads and people. Camels are laden with loads larger than could be carried in the bed of a small pick-up truck. People from societies where the major association with animals is through pets and where stringent laws regulate animal treatment often find the sight of working animals in Egypt upsetting. These animals are necessary to ease the human burden in a country that is heavily labor intensive.

Other animals seen frequently in and around the streets include stray cats and dogs. It is easy to figure out which cats and dogs belong to the streets. They look scruffy, scraggly, and gnarly. Stray animals hang around docks, hotel entrances, alleys, and restaurants – anywhere they might find food. Cats serve a good purpose by keeping the rodent population down. They can frequently be seen wandering around tables or on rafters in restaurants.

Expatriates who are not thrilled with their assignments in Egypt sometimes refer to stray dogs as "tickets." Many of these animals carry fleas, ticks, and diseases, including rabies. An expatriate who has been bitten by a stray dog can frequently get his company to send

Never feed stray animals as this tourist is doing. Rabies is common among strays.

him home for medical treatment or even reassignment, since it is not likely the animal had been vaccinated against rabies and it is usually unlikely a specific animal could be identified. Therefore, stray animals can be the expatriate's "ticket" out of an unhappy situation.

The compulsion to cuddle animals and help weak, helpless animals inclines some people to feed or pet stray animals. Most of the strays are around people enough that they are quite docile. Many will even come up to you and rub against your leg. Not all of them are docile, and one never knows which is which. Try not to let your compassion for the strays overcome your common sense.

SHOPPING

Shopping is at the same time one of the most fun things and one of the most frustrating things you can do in Egypt. Egypt has two kinds of shopping areas: modern and traditional. In the better parts of Cairo and Alexandria, modern boutiques and stores abound with the newest European fashions and Western goods.

The rest of Egypt is full of traditional small shops and fairly big stores that sell everything from toothpaste to coffeepots and batteries. They are in every nook and cranny. Major department or discount type stores, such as those found in Europe or the United States, do not really exist in Egypt. Omar Effendi's, located in most big cities, is an Egyptian counterpart to a Western department store.

As mentioned previously, markets or souks are easily accessible in all towns and cities. In stores and markets where you see printed price signs, for example in the windows, prices are set. You don't bargain in these places. If you are in doubt as to whether a place you are shopping in has fixed prices or bargaining, just ask. Sometimes shops have both fixed price items and bargaining.

Bargaining

Egyptians love to shop and bargaining is a national art form! Bargaining is a challenge that makes shopping really fun. It also gives you a great opportunity to get to know local people and their ways. Egyptians will bargain for everything from carpets to gold to trinkets to bottled water, cigarettes, and popsicles. I will briefly describe a typical process, but remember this is only a general guideline. Develop your own negotiating style and get into the spirit of Egyptian shopping.

First, you will, of course, see something you want. So you ask the price. The shopkeeper gives you a price that is the "first price." Depending on the product, this may be as much as 500% what the shopkeeper expects to get. More expensive items tend to have a lower mark-up.

Next, you can try telling the vendor you were "just looking." At this point, he will typically either ask you what you are willing to pay or give you a second or "good price." If you really don't want the product, tell him so. If, after several attempts, the shopkeeper won't take no for an answer, you can offer an "insult" price. An "insult price" is something so ridiculously low that you know and he knows you do not expect to get the item.

If, on the other hand, you actually would like to purchase the item, offer a price of say 20% of what the "first price" was. This process can have several iterations, so that before you finally agree on a price you may go through second and third or more prices before you get to a "best price." Some sellers will go directly to a "best price" after the first price if they feel you are a seasoned bargainer. Others just like the game.

Local, neighborhood bargaining or bargaining with a shop owner/keeper with whom you have an established relationship is one thing. Any time you shop in tourist areas is quite another. Shopping with local establishments where you know people will not present the problems outlined below for tourist areas.

Shopping in tourist areas can be a traumatic experience, at best. Unfortunately, you will probably shop in these areas at some time or other since tourism pervades so much of the Egyptian economy. Even if you are an expatriate living in Egypt, in tourist areas you are just another "foreign tourist" who is fair game. This is where you will typically run the gauntlet of vendors accosting you with all kinds of come-on statements and queries. They can be terrible pests! It is extremely frustrating when you say no and the hawker refuses to accept your answer, then proceeds to follow you or grab your arm to "escort" you into his shop. If a vendor grabs your arm, feel free to pull it away and tell him, very firmly, not to touch you. Vendors know they should not touch you and would never consider it proper to grab an Egyptian, especially a woman.

The best way to walk through tourist areas, such as the famous Khan el-Khalili Bazaar, relatively unassailed or unhassled, is to develop a posture that gives the appearance you know where you are going and what you are doing. Impossible at first, but easy to distinguish by shopkeepers after you have been there a few times.

A vendor at a typical tourist gauntlet. If you show interest be prepared for some insistent attention.

Don't answer queries or respond to statements made as you walk among the alleys (unless, of course, you actually want to go in to price or purchase merchandise). Foreign women often hear comments such as, "Darling, I've been looking for you all my life." Or, "Darling, I'm what you have been looking for all your life." There is a compelling tendency to make a curt or snippy response. Do not give in to the temptation. If you give any acknowledgment, you will be followed for ages, with the vendor sometimes increasing the suggestiveness of comments.

If you want to somehow politely acknowledge a "nice" shopkeeper's plea to look at his goods, you can refuse to make eye contact or speak, but, with your arm by your side, and hand facing the ground, wave the hand back-and-forth keeping the palm facing the ground. Most will leave you alone after that.

Gold

Shopping for gold requires a special comment. Egypt is known for its gold shops. Gold sold is usually 18, 21, or 24 carats. Only rarely will you ever find anything of less quality. You should see a little scratch or nick on each piece of jewelry made with Egyptian gold. This is actually a government tax stamp. The stamp is used to certify the quality of the gold and that appropriate government tax has been paid on the gold used in the jewelry.

Finding a good gold merchant is not difficult if you know a little about how to shop for gold. The most reputable gold merchants are always willing to weigh the gold and show you the scale to verify the weight. If a merchant tells you all of their gold is sold by the piece, not weight, theirs may or may not be a good place to buy. Tell them that you want them to weigh the piece anyway because you want to know how much gold is in the piece. Then you can gauge their price by what you feel is an appropriate amount to pay per gram. Some very small pieces are sold only by the piece and are only rarely negotiable.

Current gold prices are printed daily in most newspapers. The price you should pay revolves around this rate even though the gold in the jewelry you are buying may have been purchased at another rate. The real negotiating area of gold prices revolves around the cost of workmanship in the piece. The following is just an example because the price of gold fluctuates, but should give you a general feel for how to bargain for gold.

If the published price for 18 carat gold is, for example, 32 Egyptian pounds per gram with the tax stamp, you should expect to pay somewhere in the range of 40–45 Egyptian pounds per gram for a finished piece of jewelry. Unless the piece has very intricate work-manship, you should never pay more than about 10–15 Egyptian pounds per gram over the going rate for Egyptian gold – many times less. Italian gold is also popular in Egypt, but the cost is generally higher per gram than Egyptian gold.

Fruits, Vegetables, Breads and Sweets

Fruit and vegetable stalls along Cairo streets provide you with not only some of the best tasting products anywhere, but with a visual smorgasbord.

In stall after stall or in small shops, proud shopkeepers display fruits and vegetables at the peak of ripeness. Fruits and vegetables are not picked green and stored for days or weeks before being transported to market as they are in many Western societies. Produce you see at Egyptian souks may well have been picked the day before and brought by truck or donkey cart to the market overnight. Fresh warm bread and sweet pastries make your mouth water as you walk among the stalls of souks or meander into the corner bakery. Try them. They taste as good as they smell!

Duty Free Shopping

Before leaving the airport, most people stop in the duty free shops for last minute purchases. A less well known aspect of duty free shopping in Egypt is that there are several branches of Egypt Free Shops in Egypt. People entering the country are allowed to purchase products at these shops for up to one month after entering Egypt. Some items are good value and others can be bought less expensively at many of the local shops. It just depends on what you are looking for. You will need your passport and maybe your air or ferry post ticket to purchase items in these shops.

Additionally, Port Said is a duty free zone and many Egyptians go there to purchase products that would be more expensive elsewhere. Port Said shopping is not as good as it was in the past, so unless you are planning on making some major purchases, it may not be worth going there just for shopping. It is, on the other hand, a delightful city and worth the visit if you have time. Buses run from Cairo several times per day and a daily excursion to Port Said, for whatever reason, is quite reasonable.

Alcohol

A word on alcohol is pertinent at this point for one very good reason – duty free stores are the easiest and least expensive place to buy imported liquor. Like many other Muslim countries, Egypt does allow alcohol purchase and consumption within its borders but public drunkenness is not acceptable behavior under any circumstances in Egypt.

Most Muslims do not drink alcohol. Seasoned foreign business professionals neither drink alcohol in the presence of their Muslim associates nor serve alcohol in their homes when entertaining locals. If you drink alcohol, it is most prudent to do so in the confines of your home, hotel room, or in a cabaret in the absence of your Egyptian colleagues and friends. You will gain more respect from your Egyptian colleagues if you follow this behavior (even though it is certainly not required in all situations) due to your perceived understanding and respect for their religion and ways.

Sometimes my Egyptian friends who have traveled outside the Middle East think all Westerners drink alcohol and wish to show their knowledge of Western behavior and cultural practices. To make visitors feel welcome, a few Egyptians will offer you alcohol or even serve it with dinner. Again, although it is not required, you will gain more respect if you politely decline.

Some of the oldest known beer recipes come from the hieroglyphics of ancient Egypt. Contemporary Egyptian beer, Stella Local and Stella Export, are readily available at many restaurants, as are some imported beers. Egyptian wines, some of which are quite tasty and others not very good, are also available at many places in Egypt.

Buying imported liquor is easiest and cheapest at duty free shops. Otherwise, count on it being very expensive. Imported liquor is served by the glass at better hotels and restaurants throughout Egypt, where drinks are typically quite expensive. You can also buy imported liquor from the few major liquor stores, but be sure to ask specifically for imported liquor and check the label carefully.

There are a few small stores located throughout Cairo that sell liquor. Many of the local liquors have labels that look just like those of imported liquors with the exception that one word on the label may be different. An example is the substitution of the word "Waller" on the local variety for the word "Walker" on one famous brand of imported liquor. Avoid purchasing these imitations, as the contents bear no resemblance to their famous imported counterparts.

Although I have never confirmed the rumor, local folklore suggests that the imitation liquors can cause blindness. Confirmed deaths and severe illness have occurred as a result of alcohol poisoning from these products. This was because the principal component of the bottles' contents was rubbing alcohol. Some of the local, cheap liquors have very unusual smells and tastes, reminiscent of what could be a combination of perfume and formaldehyde. Since people scrounge through garbage for empty used foreign liquor bottles, which are then recycled to bottle local mixtures, break all old liquor bottles before you dispose of them to help eliminate this hazard.

– Chapter Four –

THE EGYPTIAN PEOPLE

RELIGION

If you do not understand the basic beliefs of Islam and the important effect religion has on the life and actions of all Egyptians, I firmly believe you are destined to never understand anything that goes on around you in Egypt. I say this even though there are some six to seven million Coptic Christians living in Egypt. It is estimated that 94–96% of the population of Egypt is Muslim, therefore much of the government and everyday life of all Egyptians (as well as foreign residents) are affected by this important aspect of life.

The word Islam means "having peace with God" or "submission to God." A Muslim is a follower of Islam. Do not confuse the term Muslim with the term Arab – they are not synonymous. Muslims inhabit all parts of the globe and may or may not be Arab. An Arab may be a Muslim, a Christian, a Jew or an atheist. *Allah* is the Arabic word for God. When people invoke the name of Allah, it is often stated as follows: "In the name of Allah, the Compassionate, the Beneficent." This is also the phrase you will see printed in Arabic at the beginning of many letters or publications in the Islamic world.

The *Qur'an* (also spelled Koran), or holy book of Islam, represents the literal word of God as revealed to the Prophet Mohammed (peace be upon him) through the Archangel Gabriel. When the name of the Prophet Mohammed is said or written, it is customarily followed by the phrase "peace be upon him" as shown in the previous sentence. The Prophet's "sayings" or *hadith* supplement the Qur'an as a guide to the correct conduct and behavior of Muslims. The *Hadith* includes reported sayings, deeds, and approvals of the Prophet Mohammed. This code is called the *Sunna*, literally translated to mean the "Beaten Path."

Muslims go to worship at a mosque; however, they may pray anywhere – in a house, an aircraft, outside. It is preferable to pray in a congregation, but a Muslim may pray anywhere in the world, alone or with others. Friday is the Holy Day for Muslims, so Egypt's "weekend" is Friday and Saturday, rather than Saturday and Sunday as is commonly practiced in the West.

Before I explain the basic principles of Islam (and please remember I do not represent myself as an Islamic scholar), I think I should point out an aspect of Islam probably most difficult for non-Muslims to understand. Muslims do not partition life as Westerners do into religion on the one hand, and life, work, and government on the other. This is because Islam is considered to be a total way of life. This fact is particularly difficult to understand for persons coming from countries with a strong heritage of separation between religion and the state. Church and state simply cannot be separated in the minds of average pious Muslims – both are indispensable and mutually supplementary.

The principal food restrictions among Muslims are not difficult. Islam does not allow Muslims to eat certain items, such as pork and its by-products. Muslims should also avoid alcohol. To some people, even handling alcohol is objectionable.

That being said, let's look at some of the important Islamic principles that guide the life of a believer.

- Most importantly, "There is no God but God." God is the One and the Only God. Jews, Christians, and Muslims are called the "People of the Book," the Book referred to being the Old Testament. However, Muslims reject the idea of the Trinity or any idea that implies there is more than one God, believing Jesus was a Prophet, but not God incarnate as believed by Christians.

- Muslims believe God has sent several Messengers or Prophets through the ages. The Prophets of Judaism and Christianity, such as Noah, Abraham, Moses, David, and Jesus, are also Prophets of Islam. However, importantly in Islam, Mohammed is believed to be the final Prophet or Messenger of God.

- Muslims believe God created unseen creatures such as angels for special missions.

- Muslims believe there is a Day of Judgement when all people throughout history are brought before God for accounting, punishment, and reward.

- In Islam, prayer is to God and only God and is made by the individual with no intermediaries.

- There is no "Original Sin" in Islam. Humans are born free from sin, and it is only after they reach puberty and after they commit a sin that they are charged for their mistakes. Individuals can take responsibility for their own sins. They cannot take responsibility for the sins of others. The door to forgiveness by God is always open through repentance.

The Five Pillars of Islam

Five basic duties are required of the believer in Islam. These duties are typically called the "Five Pillars" of Islam because they form the foundation of the House of Islam. The Five Pillars are:

1. **The confession of faith or affirmation of the creed** *(Shahada):* "There is no God but God, and Mohammed is the Messenger of God."

2. **Prayers** *(Salat):* Muslims are required to pray five times daily, facing in the direction of Mecca, the holiest city in Islam. The times for prayer are dawn, noon, mid-afternoon, dusk, and after dark.

3. **Fasting** *(Saum): Ramadan,* the month of the Prophet's first revelations, is the month of fasting for Muslims. Many rules regulate *Ramadan,* but basically all sane adults are obligated to fast between dawn and dusk during the month of Ramadan each year. Children are not required to fast until they reach a certain age, however children are encouraged to fast when feasible. Certain people and people living under certain circumstances are excused from fasting, although some situations require that the individual make up for time missed fasting at a later time. As a general rule of thumb, the following people are excused: travelers; the insane, retarded, or mentally impaired; invalids; and pregnant women and nursing mothers.

   One of two religious celebrations *(Eid)* occurs at the end of the month of Ramadan – the Eid of Fast-Breaking *(Eid el-Fitr).* The second major celebration, the Eid of Sacrifice *(Eid el-Adha),* is in remembrance of the sacrifice to be by Abraham of his son.

   The month of Ramadan shifts each year with respect to the Gregorian (civil) calendar. This is due to the fact that the Islamic calendar is a lunar calendar based on 354 days. Leap years have 355 days with the extra day added to the last month. The Islamic calendar began in the "year of the Hejira," or A.H. 1, which was the year the Prophet Mohammed moved from Mecca (Makkah) to Medina to escape religious persecution. A.H. 1 corresponds with the year AD 622 of the Gregorian calendar. In the 30 years of the Islamic calendar's cycle, eleven years are leap years. With the exception of leap years, the twelve months beginning with the New Year have alternately 30 and 29 days.

4. **Almsgiving, a tax or gift** *(Zakat):* It is the responsibility of all Muslims to give not less than 2.5% of their earnings, savings, and gold and silver jewelry (or its cash equivalent) to the community each year to help the poor. A different rate is levied for agricultural produce and cattle.

5. **Pilgrimage** *(Hajj):* Each Muslim is required to perform a pilgrimage to Mecca at least once in a lifetime if means are available.

HONOR, FAMILY, AND FAMILY HONOR

Never discount the value of honor in Egyptian society. Honor denotes respect, admiration, or esteem for another. It can be seen as a right or as due. Intricate interactions among honor, family, and family honor constitute some of the most important facets affecting Egyptian life.

In Egypt, an individual's honor cannot be separated from that of his/her family. As such, the actions of one family member bear directly on the reputation of all other family members. This concept is rather different from much of Western belief. In the West, an individual's reputation may well be viewed as their personal responsibility and can frequently be separated from the reputation of his/her family. For example, in the West a brother is not usually held directly responsible for his sister's behavior and/or reputation. In Egypt, the situation differs. Any behavior on the part of an individual reflects strongly on the family. Behavior of any family member is held to be the direct responsibility of the family. For example, the brother, father and all other family members bear direct responsibility for the actions of a woman, perceived actions of a woman, or any action directed toward a female family member. It is for this reason, among others, that family members concern themselves intimately with the actions of all family members.

Honor has so many implications in Egyptian life that it would be impossible to discuss them all. So I will discuss a few of the many intricately interwoven aspects of honor existing in Egyptian society.

First, honor means a code of integrity, dignity, and pride. Honor, in a general sense, applies to both the feeling and the expression of the sentiment. Throughout Egypt, feelings of honor find expression in everyday language and demeanor. For example, Egyptians are overwhelmingly concerned with demonstrating their hospitality and generosity. Dignity and pride express themselves in all aspects of dress, manners, language, business, attitudes and behavior. In daily life, Egyptians demonstrate pride and honor for their religious, political, social, and ancient heritage – in other words, their culture.

Understanding how appearance relates to honor requires using a broad perspective of how appearance integrates with behavior to Egyptians. Outward appearance, i.e., how you are dressed, your grooming, etc., is very important, most especially to upper-class Egyptians. They strive to appear well dressed and groomed at all times and cannot fathom why anyone would want to appear otherwise. As a result, dress appears to be a bit more formal than is common in the West. For example, casual dress in Egypt more closely relates to what is termed "dressy casual" in the United States. What does this concern for appearance mean for you? Well, it means that you will also be judged by your public appearance. While you may prefer ragged jeans and sloppy shirts, appearing in public dressed like this gives a bad impression. You will be judged to have little pride, thus honor, in your personal appearance.

Second, honor very importantly involves personal integrity. A person's word, honesty, and good character are hallmarks of an individual's integrity, thus the family's honor. Trustworthiness, as evidenced through honesty and good character, are critical to developing both personal and business relationships throughout Egypt.

I was reminded of the importance of honor during a discussion with a friend. When I mentioned that I wanted to bring some colleagues to Egypt, my friend reminded me: "You know I can help them, but I do not know these people. I know you very well and trust you. You must be certain they are right for this – it's a matter of honor, you know." Acknowledging my trustworthiness was indeed a great compliment and a great responsibility. Needless to say, I took a huge gulp of air and began pondering to myself whether I knew these people well enough to place my honor, indeed my integrity, on the line.

It is through personal honor that deference behavior comes into play. Outsiders often wonder why Egyptians seem to defer to others at times when foreigners customarily would not. Deference reflects respect. It is a courteous regard for another person that often takes the form of yielding to his/her decisions or wishes. In other words, deference is an honorable way Egyptians use to show appropriate respect for someone in a perceived higher position, authority, or who might be deserving of great respect for other reasons.

Two circumstances come to mind when I think of respect and deference in Egypt. While it is impossible to think of all the situations where respect/deference behavior might appear, hopefully the following examples will give you an elementary understanding of how this works. The easiest example is with age: Egyptians respect their elders. They rise when an older person enters or leaves a room. They defer to the elder person's opinion, especially in public. One would never contradict an elder in front of others. In fact, a principal requirement of "good" children is to respect their elders.

Second, in the workplace, social setting or in trade, Egyptians tend to defer to someone perceived to be in a higher social, political, or bureaucratic position. Subtle acts of deference abound in all sorts of human interactions. Expressing opinions in the presence of a "superior" is not done. Coming from a culture where expression of one's opinion is highly valued, at first I found this quite disconcerting and

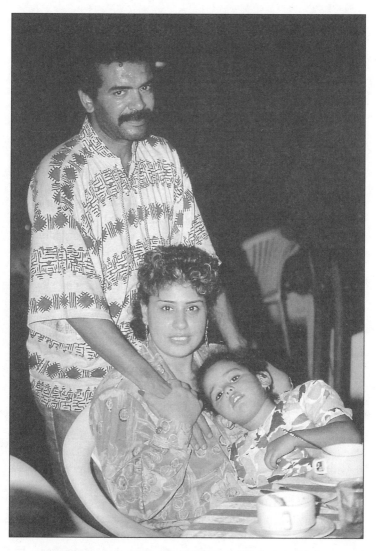

Egyptians value marriage and take great pride in their families.

could not understand such restraint. After all, if you had an opinion, why not express it? The reason is because honorable people in Egypt would never consider showing this type of disrespect to their peers or superiors. The person present with the most perceived social power should be the spokesperson, the one to express an opinion. I have noticed this often at business meetings. Frequently persons who perceive their position to be below another will not express opinions in the company of the person above them. They might express their ideas to you individually, but if an opinion is presented publicly, the person of the highest rank will usually present it unless that person refers the question to an assistant. By the way, it does not matter whether the person in the superior position is a male or female.

Subtle mannerisms of the person in the lower position reflect his or her acknowledgement of status with regard to the other individual. For example, when asked a question, there might be a slight hesitation before answering or even a non-answer to indicate that the person feels he or she should not be answering the question. You may also observe eye shifting or position shifting as a sign of discomfort. By the way, you will also get some of the same responses when you broach an inappropriate topic, so sometimes it is difficult to determine which situation prevails.

Next, women in the company of a male may find that upon asking a question, the answer is then given to the man as if they were not standing there. Alternatively, if an Egyptian man wants to get an answer from a woman, he may well address the question not to her, but to the man she is with. Western women tend to find this action demeaning – an action of deferring to male superiority. Depending on the circumstances, this kind of behavior more appropriately represents a sign of respect.

Finally, an extremely important form of honor relates to a woman's chastity or reputation for chastity. "Appearance" applies not only to the way a person looks, but also to "how things seem." How things "seem to be" can be much more important than actual facts. If a situation does not seem or appear to be appropriate, then it may be judged to be inappropriate. Any behavior or suggestion of behavior that compromises or "seems" to compromise a woman's reputation for chastity is extremely serious. Gossip also comes into play here. The way I have had it explained to me is as follows. If, for example, a woman stopped to talk with a man, it is likely that someone might see her. That someone would then tell someone else. By the third or fourth translation, the woman was at the man's home alone with him. By the time all the gossip was through the town or village, this man made her pregnant. The woman's reputation could then be ruined over nothing more than a casual conversation. Although this extreme example is less likely in Cairo, most communities even in Cairo continue to be quite closed and subject to this kind of concern.

Another example, which may seem quite innocent in the eyes of foreigners, involves men and women being alone in a room. A man should not be in a closed room alone with a woman who is not his wife because this could give the appearance of compromising the woman's respectability. If you (a male) drop by a friend's house without an appointment, you might find the woman of the house (if her husband is out) either will not answer the door or will yell through the door that no one is home. This is because it would not give the proper appearance, would not seem appropriate, for a woman to invite you into her house without her husband or other relatives present. I learned this very quickly when inviting a male Egyptian friend to join some of my colleagues in a discussion in my hotel room one afternoon. He would not come into the room, but placed a chair just outside the door in order not to give the wrong appearance and risk compromising our reputations.

Incidents of "honor killings," the murder of women for reasons of family honor, have been given a lot of international press in the past few years. The prevalence of "honor killings" is quite low in Egypt. In the event they occur, punishments tend to be less stringent than in the case of murders for other reasons.

DIVERSITY

Racism as known in the West does not occur in Egypt. This is not to say that social status distinction and even differential access to positions or power does not exist. What I am saying is that the distinction or discrimination that does exist is not based on skin color or "race" as commonly perceived in the West. Skin color may be judged on aesthetic grounds to be more or less attractive, but is not considered important in establishing one's social status.

In describing themselves and the people around them, most Egyptians more or less acknowledge the following distinct groups: Egyptians, Bedouins, Arabs (people from the Arabian Peninsula), other Middle Easterners (usually by country), and foreigners (usually by country). Several sub-categories are recognized within the group generally called Egyptian. This can be viewed as "ethnic" group distinction in some senses because people are assigned to these groups based on some common characteristics that distinguish them. However, in Egypt, people do not generally recognize the term "ethnic group." Instead, people are merely referred to as being in different "groups." The most frequent group distinction occurs simply between Muslims and Copts. Nubians and Bedouins constitute somewhat more distinct groups, although they also fall within the general grouping of Muslims.

When plans for building the Aswan High Dam began in the 1960s, President Nasser was the first to use the term "Nubian" to refer to all the dark-skinned, non-Arabic speaking peoples living between Aswan and the Sudanese border (now called "Old Nubia"). With the exception of a small group of migrants and few tribal leaders, the people from Old Nubia very rarely interacted with or were exposed to other Egyptians (and vice versa) until resettlement moved them north of Aswan in 1963. Prior to that time, if the people now called Nubians felt any common identity with one another, it was probably only based on shared grievances against the Egyptian government. Today, Nubians are a recognized ethnic group, though many of the distinctions and barriers that separated them from other Egyptians have lessened or disappeared.

The Bedouins (traditionally nomadic, but now both nomadic and settled) are perhaps the most distinct, though very small, group of Egyptians. Nomadic Egyptians live, to some extent, outside the confines of traditional Egyptian life and law. Bedouins maintain their ethnic distinction through marriage patterns, lifestyle, and tradition.

SOCIAL CLASS, POWER, AND WEALTH

Social class is the most important delimiting factor in Egyptian society, more so than any type of ethnic designation. Although social class and ethnic distinction overlap somewhat, social class structure determines access to power and position. Therefore, recognition of existing social class structure is what is important to Egyptians and to you in establishing relationships within Egypt. Probably 98–99% of the population falls within the lower and middle classes, with the rest occupying what can be termed an elite or upper class. Pragmatically, this means if you move to Egypt on a business or academic contract, you may be conducting business or socializing with only a very limited segment of the population in this realm of your life. At the same time, most of the people you see around you, and with whom you will interact daily, definitely reflect the poorer and less politically powerful majority of the population.

People in the United States prefer to see themselves as a "mobile, classless" society in which determination and hard work designate one's ultimate social position. A poor person, through diligence and hard work, can become president. In the United Kingdom, however, social position more closely affiliates to birth. This can be seen by the fact that people often know their "social class" and in the continuance of distinctions between "royalty," "nobility," and "commoner."

Egypt's social structure is somewhere between those of the United States and the United Kingdom. Importantly, no royalty or nobility classes exist in Egypt. On the other hand, very distinct social class differences delineate everyday life and potential opportunity through-out Egypt. Revolution and elections notwithstanding, a relatively small group of old, very influential families still control the majority of wealth and power within Egypt.

Most social scientists characterize Egyptian society into three basic social classes that correspond more or less with socioeconomic status – upper, middle, and lower classes. Intragroup distinctions exist within each of these classes. This classification probably will work for you in most situations. In Egypt, status is more a case of family heritage than income. Egyptian society is quite inflexible, with little or no social mobility. Members of each class tend to socialize only within their group. Almost no cross-class marriages occur. As a result, though persons may amass wealth, gain an education or both, they will not move from one class to another.

Upper-class individuals, as a total group, enjoy significantly better access to position and education than do members of the middle or lower classes. But even within this class, certain individuals have easier access. These people more often occupy higher ranking political or intellectual positions than do other members of the upper class.

Many upper middle-class individuals actually amass a great deal of wealth. However, as mentioned, acquisition of wealth does not provide a basis for moving one from the middle to the upper class – neither does education. Although members of the middle class increasingly receive a university education, their social position, vis-à-vis the upper class, remains constant. A university education certainly provides more opportunities for upward mobility within the middle class and may well increase a person's intragroup standing. University education also provides greater opportunities to migrate for work and achieve distinction in other countries.

The majority of Egyptians fall into the lower class. These people are distinguished by low educational levels and poverty. Members of this class have very little real opportunity for social mobility, though the hardworking and clever among them do improve their family's

Traditional stone carvers – class distinctions are clearly defined between Egyptians and dictate the terms of social interaction.

living conditions. Rapid population growth among this group has led to greater migration to the cities for work as family farm land is filled. Most frequently they occupy low paying positions since they are by and large unskilled. Little difference is apparent to the observer as members of this class are among the poorest in the country. Increasingly, members of the lower class achieve a secondary level education. Most still receive little education above the primary level and illiteracy levels (besides being able to write their name) continue to be quite high among this group.

Social gatherings tend to be among social status peers; rarely would one see a lower- or middle-class individual invited to a reception or dinner given by an upper-class individual at their home. Therefore, deference behavior tends to disappear or at least become less apparent in these settings. Respect due to age, of course, always applies. Certainly, it is appropriate to invite members of different social classes to your home for various events. However, whatever you do, do not mix people from different classes at a social gathering. Inviting your driver to join a function with your boss or a high ranking official would embarrass both guests.

Even within a grouping of social class peers, different relative status may still be represented within the group. For example, a high ministerial or elected official might attend a formal dinner or reception. While among members of the same social class (the upper class), this relatively higher ranking person would still receive deference and respect from members at the gathering to acknowledge his or her distinct position.

Sometimes it is difficult for foreigners to ascertain just who represents the higher rank except by quietly observing group actions. You can count on the fact that relative rank or status is well known among the Egyptians. In fact, depending on the circumstances, you may find you are the object of deference from people at a gathering because of your foreign status. This may simply reflect Egyptians' value for hospitality and honesty or it may be a sign of recognition of your perceived importance. For example, since only high ranking or wealthy Egyptians typically travel abroad, your very presence in Egypt signifies to many Egyptians that you must also be rather high ranking and wealthy. Deference to your perceived position then follows logically in their world view.

FAMILY

Life in Egypt revolves around the family. Family concerns often assume greater significance than business relationships. It would not be uncommon for someone to cancel a business meeting because some pressing family matter took greater precedence.

All Egyptians seem to love children. One of the first things I noticed in Egypt was that children were everywhere. There seem to be few public places where you won't find children. When women shop or go visiting, the custom is to bring all the children regardless of their ages. Traditionally the mother assumes major responsibility for assuring that children are reared properly. Because of this, many people think fathers are not close to their children. My observation has been that fathers often fondly hold small children and are frequently seen with them in public. As children age, fathers apparently bond more closely with their sons with regard to career and responsibility roles. Daughters become more closely aligned with their mother's role as they age. Mothers remain an important figure in their sons' lives at all ages.

Traditionally, the Egyptian standard was to live in the extended family setting comprising usually three generations in the same household. This is still the preferred living arrangement among most Egyptians, but as crowding forces more people to migrate to urban areas to work, family living arrangements have dispersed somewhat. Unless they must migrate for work or education, most unmarried children remain in the family home until they get married. Very rarely do single women move away from their family residence unless it is to another family member's home.

Traditional family size is rather large in Egypt by Western standards. Preferred family size seems to be decreasing somewhat. Many people I meet say that they would prefer to have only two or three children rather than eight, nine or more, which was customary in the previous generations. Recent efforts by government sponsors to provide family planning to Egyptians has been met with mixed success. Some people judged limiting family size to be against their religion. Since the highest Islamic authority in the country has announced that it is not against Islam, more people are moving to control family size through various contraceptive means.

COMPLEMENTARY ROLES FOR MEN AND WOMEN

Most Egyptians view men's and women's roles as complementary. Each person in the household has rights and responsibilities based on age and gender. Egyptian women are traditionally responsible for the household, whereas men are responsible for working and providing money for the family. Increasing urbanization with its shift from an agrarian lifestyle throughout Egypt challenges traditional ways of life. Women among the lower classes increasingly find it necessary to work in the labor market or in small entrepreneurial enterprises. This is frequently insulting to the family male and often results in increased family friction and violence. It is also degrading to many women, who rather than seeing an opportunity for personal expansion, perceive working to be a necessity which keeps them from fulfilling their expected responsibilities for the family and home.

Lower- and lower middle-class women usually get work in the service industry, for example, as hotel maids or restaurant servers. Upper middle-class people are also on the move. Among this group, males and females now often receive a university education and work outside the home, thereby expanding opportunities for both partners.

In Upper Egypt, women rarely work in the fields as is seen in the Delta region. The main reason is that farming in Upper Egypt is very small scale, whereas in the Delta there are larger farms where people from villages go to work for wages.

Although nothing is cast in stone, usually the eldest female occupies the role of senior person responsible for the household whereas the senior male provides for the family (or their portions of the extended family). If the father dies, usually the remaining parent continues to head the household, even though many responsibilities pass to the oldest son if the father passes first and the son is of an appropriate age. If the mother dies first, one of the daughters may assume many of the responsibilities of the household for their father's wellbeing. If the children are all grown and married, the remaining parent may move in with the family of one of the children or may remain alone if none of the married children live in the family household. Upon the death of both parents, responsibility for younger siblings and/or grandparents generally transfers to the eldest son.

EDUCATION

Education is highly valued among upper- and middle-class Egyptians as well as among the Nubians. Primary education, though technically required for all children, is not enforced uniformly throughout the country. Education is often still seen as a luxury to poor Egyptians since often children are needed to help with family economic endeavors. Among farming families, boys assist their fathers in farming activities while girls assist their mothers with household responsibilities. Other children work in trades, such as carpet weaving, to provide both a future trade occupation and supplementary family income. It seems that no matter where you are in Egypt, regardless of time of day or year, children herd animals, perform household or farm duties, or work in and around the various tourist shops.

Primary education is compulsory in Egypt and is a high government priority, yet many of the poorest children still do not attend school regularly because they are needed to help with family economic endeavors.

Sometimes only selected children get educated. Among farming families, parents often send only the oldest male children to school on a fairly regular basis. They believe these children must be somewhat educated in order to be able to get manual and other unskilled jobs in the urban areas.

Poor farming families educate only some of the children because of their values and expectations. Young girls are not perceived to need an education because it is most commonly assumed they will marry and bear household responsibilities typical of women in their villages. For boys, it is different. Farm land can only be divided so many times and still support the needs of families. This means that all of a family's male children cannot be provided land for farming after they marry. Logically, then, some of the male children must acquire some other means of supporting their future families. For example, if farm land is only sufficient for one child to inherit, often the youngest male is selected to continue the family farming tradition and assume responsibility for the parents in their old age. Thus, this child is the least likely to be perceived to need an education. Of course, if there is sufficient land, families may perceive less need to educate children since they will be expected to continue the family farming tradition.

Education for girls among the lower classes in urban areas is also sometimes viewed as an extravagance and unnecessary. The major exception to this is some vocational training for some girls, for example, training in basket or carpet weaving. In any event, most children from less wealthy families are expected to spend some of their daytime hours contributing to family endeavors.

Among wealthier Egyptians, the picture acquires the extreme opposite position. "The more education the better" seems to be the policy in this group for both male and female children. Education provides the route to wellbeing and progress. A university degree establishes the basis for getting that all important government or industry position. Education, including university education, is free to all Egyptians who qualify. However, all children are not selected for advancement to university candidacy. Although education is free, qualifying students may be forced to forego a university education because their families cannot afford to support them during this extended educational period.

Structurally, the Egyptian educational system is somewhat similar to the British one. Primary school extends from approximately ages six through twelve years. Upon completion, students may enter a preparatory school, which lasts an additional three years. At the end of preparatory school, students sit an exam to determine whether they may continue to secondary school. Depending upon the student's satisfactory completion of the preparatory school examination, they will be directed into either a general secondary or specialized secondary school. General secondary schools prepare students for a university education in the sciences or humanities. Specialized secondary schools prepare students for trade or technical professions. As in the United Kingdom, secondary schools are called "college."

To acquire a Secondary School Certificate, students must pass a major qualifying examination which lasts about three weeks. A national secondary qualifying examination is given annually to all students seeking certification in this area. Depending on the student's ranking nationally (and a passing grade), certain students may then proceed to university level training. A student's ranking determines not only if they will be allowed to go to university, but also in which programs they may enrol. Highest priority is placed on advancement to medical physician training. Only the highest ranking students throughout the country are eligible for medical training. Another percentage group of students is eligible for the next category of training, and so on. A student who is eligible to go to medical school is not required to take this track. However, a person with a lower ranking would not be allowed to study medicine.

Incidentally, while in the United States the term "faculty" refers to the professors of a university, in Egypt a faculty member is a student.

In addition to publicly supported schools throughout Egypt, numerous private schools exist. Some are based on the Egyptian model, while others base their curricula on the American model. If you plan to go to Egypt for a university education and are coming from the West, options are somewhat limited. If you are planning to enrol children in primary or secondary schools, you should probably make arrangements from abroad. In this event, you will most likely find the company sending you to Egypt will have listings for private schools from which to choose. The cost of private universities or other schooling will probably exceed US$10,000 for an academic year per student.

You will also find numerous facilities and/or individuals that provide tutoring services to assist students in exam preparation. If you seek intensive courses in classical or colloquial Arabic, several facilities exist which provide short-term courses at reasonable rates. At this time, the listing of private schools on the Internet is limited, but undoubtedly more and more schools will have webpages in the future from which to gain information at a distance. Alternatively, check with your Egyptian embassy, consulate office, or tourist authority for further information.

Chapter Five

COMMUNICATING EGYPTIAN STYLE

THE VERBAL DIMENSION

Arabic, the official language of Egypt, sounds strange to the native English speaker. At once it rings with a lilting melodic intonation accompanied by an alien series of guttural sounds difficult for the English speaking palate to form.

Eleven distinct languages or dialects ring out in the cacophony of sounds throughout Egypt. Cairene Arabic is the most widely understood dialect used for non-print media, both in Egypt and throughout the Arab world. It is an amalgam of Delta Arabic and Middle Egypt Arabic with borrowings from literary Arabic. Saidi or Upper Egyptian Arabic follows as the second most common dialect in Egypt. Egyptian Spoken Arabic distinguishes itself from Arabic spoken in other parts of the Arab world principally through a few consonant sounds and local colloquial phrases. Most highly educated Egyptians speak English and/or French.

Classical or Modern Standard Arabic (MSA), which is not a mother tongue, is the language of the *Qur'an*, the Islamic holy book. It is also used in most textbooks for learning written Arabic. This form of Arabic finds its greatest utility in written materials and formal speeches. Learning Classical Arabic provides an excellent basis from which to read Arabic newspapers or documents. It also forms a good platform to develop spoken Arabic, though words in spoken dialects differ as much as 50% from MSA, according to some sources.

Many tapes for learning Arabic phrases use Egyptian Arabic because it is a widely understood dialect. Since Egyptian cinema and recordings are popular throughout the Arabic-speaking world, most people who speak the language understand the normalized Egyptian Spoken Arabic (based on Cairo speech) established through the media.

Coptic, one very important language you will not hear spoken, reportedly comes from Ancient Egypt. This extinct language lives on through the liturgical language of the Coptic Christian Church. No first language speakers of Coptic exist, since the language went extinct apparently in the sixteenth century.

The large numbers of foreign tourists throughout Egypt introduce an interesting effect on communication styles. Anywhere that you find a significant tourist penetration, you will also find people able to communicate at least minimally in English, French, German, Italian, Spanish, Japanese, and probably several other languages. In tourist areas, people constantly approach the unwary stranger in a language Egyptians guess, based on the foreigner's appearance, will be understood. If you don't respond to entreaties in one language, tourism entrepreneurs simply switch languages until they find one you understand. However, in the more traditional parts of cities or in the rural areas, few people speak any language other than their native tongue.

GREETINGS AND COMMON PHRASES

Do you have to learn Arabic to get along in Egypt? Yes and no – it depends on where you are, what you are doing, who you are with, as well as how long you intend to stay. In some instances, it may prove more beneficial to understand how many Egyptians perceive some aspects of communication rather than concern yourself with total proficiency in the Arabic language.

Words possess power. As such, conversations contain frequent blessings to keep things going well. Blessings are also used to demonstrate that the speaker harbors no envy toward a person or object. Westerners commonly attribute this speaking pattern to concepts of fatalism – that one cannot control one's fate. However, another perspective is that frequent blessings actually represent efforts to control future events to some extent. For example, envy or perceived envy toward something relates to belief in the "evil eye," a belief shared by many Europeans and some North Americans. Belief in the evil eye (or just "the eye"), though common, is less pronounced among educated Egyptians. The evil eye is feared because it can bring harm to a person or thing if looked at (consciously or unconsciously) with envy. To prevent harm, and therefore the perception of envy, one should offer blessings or other statements of goodwill. Amulets, used in conjunction with religious phrases, most frequently depict drawings of eyes, open palm prints, and the color blue.

To avoid making a bad situation worse, euphemisms replace explicit references to an illness, death, or disaster. Until you can learn the local euphemism code, it is probably best to try to avoid conversations related to these types of sensitive subjects. The principal exception is describing symptoms to a doctor, which should always be explicit.

How you say something is often perceived to be as important as what you say. Egyptians speak and write with a flowery eloquence unlike English verbal or written patterns. What appears to be long-winded, repetitious dialogue should be viewed as a demonstration of the speaker's high educational level and refinement. Don't be put off by threats, promises, exaggerations, or nationalistic slogans that pepper dialogues. These are meant for effect, and again represent the speaker's language proficiency.

Certainly command of the local language gives you an advantage in daily life or business. On the other hand, since so many people in Egypt speak English, native English speakers find simple daily survival easy without fluent Arabic – especially in the major cities. If you plan to stray away from the beaten path, you will likely need a minimal command of Arabic or a translator. The respect you receive and your acceptance in the country improves considerably once you command knowledge of elementary greetings and responses. Listed below are some key everyday greetings and phrases. For a pronunciation guide, see any standard Egyptian Arabic phrasebook or the source for this information written by Margaret K. Nydell (which is listed in the recommended readings at the end of this book).

Shukran
Literally, "thank you." Probably *shukran* will be the first Arabic word you learn.

'afwan or *el 'afw*
Literally, "you're welcome;" "not at all;" or "don't mention it." Either the long or short form is an appropriate response to "thank you."

Iwa (Aywa) or *naíam*
Literally, "Yes." *Iwa* seems to be used more frequently in Egypt than *naíam*, although both are understood and accepted.

La'
Literally, "No." Used alone or in a series – *la', la', la'* is the common way to say no.

assalamu 'alaykum and *wa 'alaykum assalam*
Literally, *assalamu 'alaykum* means "peace be upon you." It is the more formal greeting for meeting new people. Literally, *wa 'alaykum*

assalam, translates to "and upon you peace." It is the appropriate response to the formal hello. This greeting seems to be used less frequently as a greeting in Egypt than other parts of the Middle East.

Marhaba

Marhaba is a more informal "hello" greeting used either between friends or when greeting a stranger, for instance in a store.

ahlan and ahlan wa sahlan

Literally, *ahlan* and its response *ahlan wa sahlan* mean "nice to meet you" or "welcome." This is the most common greeting used among friends and strangers alike in Egypt.

Ma'a ssalama and Allah yisallimak

Literally, "Go with safety" and "May God make you safe." *Ma'a ssalama* is a common goodbye phrase used when leaving someone's home or business.

Inshallah (Insha'Allah)

Literally, "God willing." *Inshallah* is used frequently in conversations. For example, when confirming that you will be at a meeting, it is common to hear something like: "I will be there at ten, *Inshallah*" or *"Bukra, Inshallah."* (Tomorrow, God willing.)

Izzayak? (to a man) or Izzayik? (to a woman)

Literally, "How are you." Notice the different form used for men and women.

alhamdu lillah

Literally, "Thanks be to God" Although there are many phrases used to say "I'm fine," this is one of the most frequently used.

Hamdillah 'ala ssalama

Literally, "Thanks be to God for your safety." This phrase is used when someone recovers from an illness or returns from a trip.

Mashallah (Ma sha' Allah)

Literally, "What God wills." This phrase is used when seeing a child or complimenting someone's health.

Ma'alish

Literally, "Never mind" or "It doesn't matter." When Egyptians translate this phrase into English, they most often say, "No problem!" *Ma'alish* is much more than a casual phrase, it actually represents a total way of looking at life's trials and tribulations. The phrase provides a whole range of responses to disappointments, frustrations, and acceptance of adversity.

SOCIAL INTERACTIONS

Warm, friendly, smiling, happy Egyptians abound throughout the country. In keeping with the tradition of hospitality, a call of "Welcome! Welcome my friend!" penetrates every exchange from well-known friend to total stranger. So why do I include sections on smiles, eye contact, and touching? Mainly it is because a smile, a touch, or eye contact at the wrong time and with the wrong person can get you into a situation you probably want to avoid. First, take a quick glimpse at common social interactions including their smiling, touching, and eye contact behavior.

In the course of normal conversation, Egyptians make intense eye contact, smile a lot, and touch each other. Look carefully – most times you will notice these interactions involve same sex interplay – especially in public. Social rules for appropriate behavior between same sex and male/female interactions differ substantially depending very slightly on the circumstances. The rules roughly fall out as follows. Don't forget these are only broad generalizations, but it should get you by until you get a feel for the territory.

It is always appropriate to smile, make intense eye contact, and even touch frequently and warmly when in same sex groups. This applies for men and women. In Egypt, the standard greeting upon seeing someone you know, whether in business or social situations, usually includes kissing first on one cheek and then the other between persons of the same sex – often while shaking hands.

Handshaking patterns tend to differ between Westerners and Egyptians. Rather than a perfunctory, strong, short handshake typical in much of the West, Egyptians tend to have a less-gripping (even limp, by American standards) handshake. Sometimes, they may continue to hold your hand long after it would seem appropriate by Western standards, but this is normal in Egypt. Both men and women shake hands but in most circumstances a man should probably wait for the woman to offer her hand in mixed company.

Since men do not typically kiss one another in many parts of Europe and the United States, this can be a little unsettling until one gets used to the practice. More shocking to the Western male, Egyptian men hold hands as they walk and talk. Contrary to some people's beliefs, holding hands among males and cheek kissing does not mean Egyptian men are homosexuals. The only comparison I can think of in Western society translates to the type of camaraderie shared by men on sports teams where traditional Western touching barriers among men tend to drop. Once you begin to get accepted in Egyptian society, an Egyptian male friend may well begin to treat you as he would an Egyptian male friend and casually take your hand as you stroll along the street. In most cases, when this happens, it should be viewed as a sign that you are beginning to be seen as an equal – not as an inappropriate overture. Never fear, a person interested in a homosexual liaison is likely to let you know in a myriad of other ways including an outright statement of intent.

Oddly, although Western women do not usually find the cheek kissing greeting with other women uncomfortable, they frequently find arm-in-arm or hand holding with women as they walk a bit unsettling. Normally Egyptian women link arms when walking to bring them closer to their companion so they can talk more easily. Again, when an Egyptian woman takes your arm in the normal course of walking, it symbolizes acceptance and friendship.

Mixed gender situations are where things can become problematic. So much of what is acceptable depends on how well you know the person and upon how familiar the person is with foreign social practices. Obviously, the more educated Egyptians accept differences in social interaction more easily without misinterpretation than do those who are not familiar with other cultures. Most social situations in which you are likely to be involved will tend to be a bit more formal than is customary in the United States. Therefore, I definitely recommend using some caution in interactions, particularly at first, until you become familiar with what is acceptable behavior. Probably the best rule to follow is to let your Egyptian colleagues or friends establish the pace of interactions. In general, the following guidelines apply.

If you are in a social situation, whether for business or at the home of a friend, and spouses are present, male-female interaction stays on a rather formal level. Smiles between men and women may appear somewhat distant though sincere. Conversations revolve around non-personal topics. Male-female touching should be limited to a handshake. Eye contact in these situations should be rather limited, but you should not appear to be avoiding looking at someone with whom you are talking as this can be interpreted as aloofness and lack of sincerity. Once you become very good friends, these types of situations become more relaxed. Rather than being the initiator of a cheek kissing greeting upon arrival or departure, just follow the Egyptian person's lead, especially in mixed company.

Men should always be somewhat reserved when interacting with Egyptian women, even with women they know fairly well. "Showing too much interest" can compromise the woman's reputation and honor, and thus the man's as well. The concept of "showing too much interest" is relative, but remember even the slightest personal attention could compromise an Egyptian woman. In most social situations, it is fairly easy for foreign men to avoid close interactions with Egyptian women because the women will generally keep fairly distant, either physically or by demeanor. Often men and women will retire into separate groups, after dinner for example, eliminating the issue. This practice also assists foreign women who might be placed in an awkward situation.

Say, for example, you are an unaccompanied man in a setting with an Egyptian man and his wife. In this situation, conversation should probably be kept at a fairly casual level. If the woman seems to not participate extensively in conversation, it is not necessary to try to involve her more in the conversation. By some standards, this might seem as if she is being ignored, but by Egyptian standards it may be perceived as normal. Follow her lead and you probably won't go wrong.

If a woman accompanies a foreign male (again in a setting with an Egyptian man and his wife), the women will probably engage in a separate conversation from the men. More commonly, after perfunctory greetings and initial conversation are over, the men or the women will retire to separate rooms for conversation.

At the dinner table or at a reception when there is a mixed group, just remember to keep the conversation very casual and never try to engage an Egyptian woman in discussions of personal issues. If you do get off on a topic that is deemed too personal or one which is inappropriate for the setting, your Egyptian host will indicate this by giving you a totally noncommittal answer or by casually changing the subject. Don't forget; topics considered as appropriate for casual conversation in the West can easily be out of bounds in Egypt.

Foreign men should never try to start conversations with Egyptian women to whom they have not been properly introduced, except as required for a business transaction. This could be interpreted as a sign of disrespect, and thus by extension risk compromising the woman's reputation. A foreign man's interest in an Egyptian woman could be interpreted (especially by less educated Egyptian men) to mean he wants the woman for his wife or worse, suggest less acceptable intentions. Unless this is what you want, it is best to avoid speaking to women who are strangers. However, should marriage be your intent, find the woman's appropriate male relative with whom you should negotiate to establish a marriage contract and proceed from there.

A foreign woman who starts a conversation with a male stranger also runs the risk of compromising her respect as well as her reputation if the conversation is for anything other than a bargaining, academic, or business type interaction. Socially acceptable behavior quite simply prevents Egyptian women from engaging unknown men in conversation. To do so, even as a foreigner, leaves you open to lewd suggestions or offers of marriage. Don't forget the goal of all Egyptians is to have a good marriage, therefore any unmarried female is fair game. Most typically, immediate marriage proposals are intended only to flatter the unsuspecting foreign woman and mean no real intent. The reasoning goes as follows: If the woman's morals were high, she would not be engaging in this type of unacceptable behavior, therefore any type of comment is okay.

While this may seem unfair, it is based on logic according to local perceptions of acceptable behavior. On the whole, average Egyptian men on the street do not have a high regard for the morals of Western women. They are, of course, basing this judgement on their own standards as compared with their limited understanding of Western women and life. For the most part, average Egyptian men have few ways of learning about Western women. Direct learning is usually gained from interactions with or observations of tourists. There they may see women drink alcohol, wear revealing clothes, or behave in other ways unacceptable for respectable Egyptian women. Indirectly, many TV programs and movies, broadcast via cable or satellite, provide another basis for judging the morals of Western women.

However, do not discount the fact that some Egyptian marriages are still arranged based on nothing more than a casual smile across a room. Additionally, some Egyptian men, especially lower middle-class men, would like nothing better than to have a foreign wife, assuming it would provide them a passport to a more affluent life. Others simply think it would improve their social standing among their peers to have a foreign wife. In her excitement for learning about everything Egyptian, one of my students pursued a conversation with a shopkeeper, asking "all about Egyptian life." Big mistake! To her surprise and embarrassment, she found herself accidentally "engaged" within about one hour of arriving in Cairo and spent the next three weeks trying to avoid her would-be suitor who was extremely persistent.

So what do you do if you really want an Egyptian husband? Well, the first thing is to meet men through an appropriate introduction, for example through business, at social clubs, at university or through friends. Second, understand the nature of courtship, the marriage contract and how it is arranged in Egypt. Third, have someone act as your intermediary, preferably a male relative or minimally an Egyptian friend who can act as your "brother," to arrange the contract.

THE VERBAL DIMENSION

In Egypt, conversations frequently involve close contact and low tones, sometimes almost at the level of a whisper. Just as frequently, conversations suddenly erupt into loud shouting matches with everyone talking at once accompanied by arm waving, table pounding, threatening gestures, and generous punctuating oaths. Boisterous dramatizations more commonly occur among males of the same age and social status who know each other well, but can also occur among total strangers.

Once when I was taking a group of Americans to a market in old Alexandria, we had an unanticipated police escort. Much to our surprise, our escort took us through traffic to the wrong place. When I began exclaiming loudly to our interpreter that we did not want to go to this place, but another, the bus screeched to a halt, my colleague departed, a crowd gathered, and there ensued a loud screaming match replete with vociferous arm waving and pointing. Next thing my group knew I was out yelling at our interpreter who then relayed my complaints in a loud voice to the escort. People sat mesmerized in their seats, shrinking at the idea that some or all of us were going to be hauled off to jail for fighting in public. Of course, it was simply conversation quite normal to the Egyptians involved.

THE NONVERBAL DIMENSION

Successful communication in Egypt requires not only the ability to communicate verbally, but also an understanding of the nonverbal aspects of communication that accompany speech. Sometimes called the silent language, paralanguage, or body language, it comprises all those hidden means of communication we convey with our presence. Nonverbal communication among Egyptians is intense and very much a sensory experience. Talking is often accompanied by gestures, touching, mutual enjoyment of warm, moist breath and smells, and piercing looks with the eyes.

GESTURES

Especially when excited, Egyptians make liberal use of gestures when talking. Listed below are some of the more common dos and don'ts concerning gestures. If you watch people closely you will also begin to notice head and facial gestures that are commonly part of communication. Since foreigners often use gestures in the wrong place or situation, it is advisable that you do not use these gestures until you are very familiar with Egyptian culture, but it is important to recognize them in order to get the full meaning of what is going on around you. You should note that most common hand gestures should be made with the right hand only – never the left.

- Most Western lewd hand or arm gestures are well understood throughout Egypt, and should not be used under any circumstances.

- Probably every tourist book in the world written about traveling in the Middle East reminds people not to cross their feet exposing the soles to people. This is an extreme insult.

- A common gesture used in the United States is to raise one's hand and make a circle with the thumb and forefinger to mean "good" or "OK." The same symbol may mean, "zero" to the French, "money" to the Japanese, or "male homosexual" in Malta. Do not use this gesture in Egypt. If you want to indicate something is OK or very good or that you are winning, it is a better bet to use the old "thumbs up" gesture by making a fist with the right hand with the thumb extending upwards.

- Pointing at people is equally insulting in Egypt as in the United States and Europe.

- Beckoning someone to come to you by holding the hand palm up, curling the forefinger several times, is considered rude and commanding. If you want someone to come over to you or to indicate that you want to talk with someone, hold the right hand up, palm facing outward, and close all four fingers back and forth to the palm.

- If you want someone to go away, hold the right hand out, palm downward, and either move it laterally back and forth or move it as if scooping something away from you. It will also be understood if you use this gesture with the right arm hanging down by your side or just slightly in front of the leg.

- If you want someone to wait, calm down, go slowly, or be patient, hold the right hand out, palm upward, touch the thumb and fingers together, and them move the hand up and down.

SPACE

Personal space is really a Western concept that is foreign to most Egyptians, especially in public. Much of this probably relates to differing concepts of the "self" as interpreted through alternative cultural perceptions. To the Westerner, "self" means all of the body, the shell of the individual, i.e., the tangible person. To the Egyptian, the "self" resides somewhere deep within the core of the shell, closely tying the individual with the more representative meanings of honor, morality, and character, i.e., the symbolic person. The way this translates into behavior is quite simple: Westerners prefer a minimum communication distance of about 18 inches, whereas Egyptians prefer 9-10 inches.

Don't be surprised if you find yourself backing up when talking with an Egyptian. I have watched conversations proceed down a hall or across a room when a Westerner could not adjust to very close proximity when talking. Closeness when talking in the United States or Great Britain is reserved for intimacy or secrets. Even when stuck in an elevator, Europeans and Americans often back as far away as possible and stop talking, petrified they may actually have to touch another person or smell their breath. Adjusting to close proximity

Bargaining over the price of a camel – personal space takes a back seat in Egypt but eye contact is important to show trust and sincerity.

with others requires time. You will probably never be completely comfortable with the typical personal space distance in Egypt, but you will adjust.

SMILES

As mentioned above, it is quite acceptable to smile and make limited eye contact in mixed-gender social circumstances among friends and acquaintances or to smile through the course of normal conversation. Of course, men should be extremely cautious to avoid smiling beyond a casual greeting smile at Egyptian women under all circumstances. Directed smiling at women you don't know may be interpreted as rude, a sexual approach and/or as an insult because it shows a lack of respect and compromises an Egyptian woman's reputation. In extreme situations, making this type of inappropriate approach could result in her male relatives' retribution for their family honor or their approach to you to establish a marriage contract (which was probably not your intent). Remember, among more conservative single Egyptians mixed-gender contact other than with close relatives rarely occurs, so smiling is a way they indicate prospective interest in a marriage.

Since foreign men's exposure to Egyptian women is likely to be more limited than foreign women's exposure to men (there are simply more Egyptian men out and about), the remainder of this section will consider women's smiling behavior. Social rules are different for women. There are certain circumstances where it is totally inappropriate for women to smile warmly at men – most especially, in public places with strangers. As much as I hate categorizing, establishing "types" of smiles is probably the easiest way to explain consequences of unwitting smiles from foreign women. Although there are huge ranges of smiles, for the sake of simplicity, I am going to categorize smiles into three types which are fairly easy to recognize: formal or polite (e.g., for business or shopping interchanges), social, and informal.

When a woman smiles warmly (with or without eye contact) at a male stranger, this means "she is interested," so a warm smile is frequently interpreted as a come-on. Coupled with the not uncommon Egyptian man's perception that Western women are "loose" or "on the make," unwary smiles can place you in an extremely awkward position. Rarely is this type of smile interpreted as a prelude to marriage. In fact, though I often advise women to be cautious in making eye contact with Egyptian men, a smile can be even more suggestive and, thus, more problematic. There is something between a full-blown smile and a frown. If you are a woman going to Egypt, practice it.

Now I am not suggesting that if you are a female you should walk around with a scowl or frown on your face. Certainly, "polite" or "distant" smiles, especially when thanking someone or asking directions with strangers is all right. But you should be careful of the "casual" smile, because casual in Egypt is not the same as casual in the West.

Broad differences in smiling behavior among cultures tend to break down as follows. People ignore strangers in public in some cultures while others do not. For example, it is rare for people to acknowledge each other at a train station, a lift or generally in public in the United Kingdom. In parts of the United States, this is also not uncommon – for example in East Coast subways. However, people from many parts of the United States tend to smile, nod, and/or say, "hello, how are you" to strangers as they walk down the street, enter an elevator, or in any situation when they are in direct proximity with another person regardless of gender. To them, it means nothing, but is simply considered a common courtesy and polite behavior. If you happen to be from an area where this latter practice is common, it will be difficult to break this habit, but break it you must if you don't want misunderstandings on a regular basis.

Since I happen to come from an area where it is considered rude to pass a stranger without some sort of greeting, I speak from considerable experience on how difficult this habit is to break. To show how important it is to curb this particular habit, however, let me give you an example of what happened to a friend on an Egyptian train. A happy, friendly beautiful American woman enjoying the thrill of being in Egypt entered a train. In doing so, she smiled brightly (with little eye contact) and politely said "Excuse me" to a man standing close to the door as she passed. Totally innocent and required behavior from her perspective, her actions were totally misinterpreted by the man. He followed her into the car, tried to start a conversation, and asked her to sit with him. She, of course, became distressed by the attention, not understanding why he was following her. According to her normal rules of behavior, she had done nothing wrong. When a colleague quickly tried to come to her rescue by telling the man to leave and that she was his daughter, the man simply asked her "father" if he could sit with her. Profuse "no's" were not accepted and the man proceeded to stand at the end of the car and stare at the woman, making her even more uncomfortable. Finally, a couple of our Egyptian male friends had to intervene to get the man to leave her alone.

EYE CONTACT

In Egypt, reading eyes is a nonverbal art form. Americans and especially northern Europeans find the intense level of gaze common in Egypt to be disconcerting and uncomfortable. Why? Because long, deep, penetrating gazing in the West generally means intimacy. In fact, depending on where you are from, direct eye contact connotes honesty, respect, disrespect, flirtation, or a sexual come-on. Among some subcultures, direct, non-prolonged eye contact means sincerity and truth. Among other groups, it is a sign of disrespect. Typically, northern Europeans are among the least comfortable with high levels of gaze during conversations. This is true for either male or female, whether in mixed or same sex groups.

Direct, semi-prolonged or intense eye contact between same or mixed sex individuals in a business meeting implies honesty and sincerity among Egyptians. This gets back to reading eyes. Most people cannot control pupil dilation when their interest is aroused. It doesn't have to be sexual interest between a man and a woman. Any kind of interest will do, for example a comment made in a business meeting which triggers interest in pursuing the business deal. Therefore, to the Egyptian, much can be learned about the honor and integrity of a person by gazing intently into the eyes.

In a society such as Egypt where men and women do not customarily have a great deal of social or verbal interaction except in school, within the family, or in conducting business transactions, eyes tell much about the character of the individual. Inadvertent, frequent eye contact can be particularly hazardous for the Western woman in non-business related settings. Even relatively brief eye contacts, especially when repeated a few times, denotes interest and might be considered coquettish, flirtatious, or an open sexual invitation. Certainly, the more educated or Westernized Egyptians accept greater latitude in eye contact than do others due to the simple fact that they have more frequent contact with outsiders and are more able to judge behavior on non-ethnocentric guidelines.

TOUCHING

As mentioned above, same sex interactions are replete with touches and gestures. Keep your hands to yourself in mixed company! Unmarried males and females simply do not touch one another, especially in public. Married people often walk arm-in-arm or occasionally hold hands when walking. Regardless of whether you are with Egyptians or other foreigners, kissing, fondling, or other public displays of intimacy are strictly taboo throughout Egypt.

Except when shaking hands, men should be careful never to touch Egyptian women except in an emergency. If she falls on the street, it is probably all right to pick her up, but remove your hands as quickly as possible. Women – if a man falls, let him get up on his own or let other men assist him as necessary. Do not intervene unless you are a doctor and the person's life or safety is at stake.

EGYPTIAN TIME

The clock reads the same in Egypt, but responses and expectations differ significantly from those in the West. Working on Egyptian time boggles the mind. Things happen when they happen – no sooner. If you are on a tight schedule, you are probably destined to suffer severe frustration. Your best bet is to simply learn to work in approximate time schedules.

I have occasionally asked friends how long it would take to walk or drive to some place nearby. Invariably the answer seems to be the same. Except on rare occasions, every place is ten minutes' walk or drive. My usual response is, "Ten Egyptian minutes or American minutes?"

I view Egyptian time as a process of: *"Yalla! Yalla!* – Wait." "Yalla!" simply means "Let's go!" or "Hurry up!" No matter how much you hurry, inevitably interminable waits follow your haste. Expect delays and adjust – it is the norm.

QUEUING

Forget you ever knew the concept, it does not happen in Egypt! Just like driving, people traffic in Egypt knows no lane markers. Only a forced queue could possibly persuade Egyptians to "wait in line."

Once I watched a number of Americans dutifully form what they perceived to be a line while waiting to get a ticket for the Metro. Totally confounded by people slipping outstretched arms with money in front of them, the Americans still waited in line. They just kept standing, unsure of what to do next. Finally, a sympathetic toll taker noticed the Americans standing there and waved them forward to sell them their ticket.

So, be assertive. Get into the spirit of how to get that burger or Metro ticket. Otherwise, you may wait a considerable time before someone takes sympathy on your plight.

PHOTOGRAPHY

You should always ask permission before taking a picture of someone you don't know. You can do this verbally, or as I often do, by getting their attention, pointing to the camera and shrugging the shoulders as if asking, "Is this OK?" Asking before snapping the shutter applies specifically when you focus in on an individual or small group of people. Of course, when taking street scene pictures, it is impossible to ask permission of all the people. In this case, use your posture to make sure no particular person feels threatened by the camera. After all, most people are quite used to seeing hundreds of tourists running around the country snapping pictures everywhere.

Women are particularly sensitive about having their pictures taken by strangers. If a woman sees you aiming a camera lens at her and does not want her picture taken, usually she will turn away. An alternative way to let the shutterbug know a picture should not be taken involves raising the hand over the face or holding the arm up towards the photographer. Some men also do not want their pictures taken. They use the same nonverbal signals, and also will occasionally shout out at you. Especially in tourist areas, people allow you to take their picture for a small tip. Again, ask. Do not offer a gratuity to a friend when taking pictures among a group, but it never hurts to ask if it is OK to take the pictures.

Photography is allowed at all antiquities, but sometimes photography tickets are required. Other areas allow photography, but no flash pictures. Still other places require special tickets for the use of video cameras.

It is against the law to take some pictures – usually politically sensitive buildings, embassies, or military installations. Also, there is still a prohibition against taking pictures of bridges, but this seems to be less enforced now than in the past. If you are in a locality where pictures are not allowed, usually there is a policeman or military person around who will tell you not to take pictures. Signs indicate a few areas where photography is banned – such as the airport.

Finally, and this is very important, never tell someone you will send them copies of the pictures unless you absolutely, positively can do so. Many people in rural areas or even at tourist sites ask if you will send them copies. Most tourists are insensitive, usually saying, "Yes, I will send them as soon as I get home." Then they go home and never communicate with anyone again. On the other hand, do not tell them, "No, I cannot send you a copy." Instead, tell them, *"Insha'Allah"* or "I will send you a picture if I can." This will be understood. It allows you to answer positively, which is appropriate, but not to feel as though you committed to action you cannot reasonably accomplish.

– Chapter Six –

CUSTOMS AND CELEBRATIONS

HOLIDAYS AND FEASTS

Friday is a public holiday in Egypt. The following dates on the Gregorian calendar are observed as official public holidays in Egypt:

New Year's Day	1 January
Union Day	22 February
Labour Day	1 May
Anniversary of the British Evacuation	18 June
Anniversary of the Egyptian Revolution	23 July
Anniversary of Suez	24 October
Victory Day	23 December

Some holidays and feasts occur on a rotating basis during the year because they are based on the Islamic calendar. Each occurs some ten to twelve days earlier every year. The Muslim holidays observed in Egypt include Mouled el-Nabi (the Birth of the Prophet Mohammed),

Eid el-Adha (to commemorate Prophet Abraham's sacrifice of his son Ishmael), Eid el-Fitr (observed at the end of the fasting month of Ramadan), and the Islamic New Year.

RAMADAN

Ramadan is a particularly important month in any Muslim country. Egypt is no exception. During Ramadan, many shifts occur in daily schedules due to the requirement to fast during this month. Instead of staying open all day, many businesses and shops shorten daytime working hours. In fact, during the month of Ramadan, things essentially shut down during the day throughout Egypt.

Egyptians do not starve themselves during Ramadan. Basically, the fast simply requires a shifting of schedule from primary activity during daylight to night-time activity. Each day the fast is broken by a large meal served shortly after sunset. During Ramadan, Egyptians who observe the fast arise before sunrise. It is customary to consume a fairly large meal before the daily fast begins. As a result of eating pattern shifts, activity patterns also shift during Ramadan. Egyptians, always prone to night-time activity, increase their nightly activity significantly during this period. Nights are used for visiting, shopping, and some business activities. Ramadan is followed by the Eid of el-Fitr, a multi-day celebration during which families gather for feasting and prayer.

During summer months, activity also picks up significantly during the evenings. Postponing activity until night avoids the worst heat of the day, but does not necessarily involve a consequent shift in eating patterns. Obviously, observing the Ramadan fast during the summer increases the length of time between meals.

As a visitor to or foreign resident in the country, you may choose not to follow the Ramadan fast. If so, you should not eat in public if it can be avoided. The major general exception to this rule revolves around tourists and some tourist establishments. Egyptians in and around the tourism industry acknowledge that many tourists to their land are not Muslim. Therefore, many seek to accommodate tourists by providing daytime meals to them throughout this period. Most commonly, only the larger hotels and tour ships accommodate tourists in this way. Even in tourist areas, access to everything is limited during the day. If you can, buy food supplies you think you will need for the next day during the preceding evening. You should count on finding restaurants, cafes, and most business establishments closed during most of the daylight hours of Ramadan.

FESTIVALS

A couple of major festivals also occur in Egypt. The Cairo International Fair takes place during the first half of March. Another interesting festival, the Sham el-Nessim (literally the "Scent of Spring"), actually traces its history back to the time of the Pharaohs. In ancient days, Egyptian men gave a lotus flower to their ladies and families took leisurely cruises down the Nile in flower decorated *feluccas*. Now, almost everyone celebrates the Sham el-Nessim by having family picnics in gardens and parks along the Nile. This traditional festival takes place on Monday following the Coptic Easter. By the way, the Coptic calendar differs from the Islamic and Gregorian calendars. As a result, Coptic Easter does not occur at the same time as Easter is celebrated in other countries.

DATING AND MARRIAGE

Courtship rituals in Egypt differ significantly from those in the West. Young men and women do not have the range of opportunities to get to know one another as they do, for example, in the United States or Great Britain. As a rule, only a small portion of the upper-class population undertakes anything that roughly corresponds to what is termed dating in the West. Even so, these relationships tend to be associated with public activities. Rarely would couples spend time alone. Unmarried couples simply do not live with one another in Egypt.

Some young people do attend discotheques, movies, social clubs, and sporting events. Access tends to be limited by both wealth and social acceptance. People who socialize at these places generally tend to be more educated, wealthier, and wear Western style clothing. Still, only an extremely small percentage of Egyptians consider it proper for young men and women to be out socially on a one-to-one basis. Western style dating relationships are frowned upon by the majority of people in Egypt. This kind of behavior is frequently seen as decadent and a sign of Western moral decay.

Negotiating Marriage

Under Islamic law, a non-Muslim man or woman has to convert to Islam to marry a Muslim. Muslim marriages involve several steps. Significant differences in each phase of marriage occur depending on geographical region and local custom. Therefore, the following represents only a general procedural pattern.

First, the potential partner is selected; this is discussed in detail below. Second, the dowry must be negotiated. This step involves settling on an appropriate dowry that the groom must give to the bride. The bride is not directly involved in these negotiations. The dowry is given to the bride's family, which is then given to the girl. The dowry usually consists of some type of durable wealth. Depending upon the economic status of the families, dowries range from some fixed amount of gold to household wares. Among Bedouins, men usually give camels for their brides. The dowry is the woman's to keep and never becomes the property of her husband. Some social scientists call the dowry a "bride price." In many ways, this is a misnomer since the dowry eventually goes to the prospective bride. The groom is not "buying" a wife. Neither is the family "selling" their daughter. Giving the bride a dowry is better regarded as a statement of good faith and intention. It does not signify a transfer of ownership, rather a transfer of responsibility. In fact, the dowry establishes the girl's independence in some regards because it means she has her own wealth.

127

The third step, which is actually the first of the two-part marriage ritual, is the signing of the marriage contract. No vows are exchanged at any step in the Muslim marriage ritual. The marriage contract is both religious and secular. It can be viewed as both in that many parts of the contract are established by Egyptian family law, which is in turn based on Islamic tradition. The marriage contract is religious in that ritual agreement of marriage rights and responsibilities constitutes an old Muslim tradition. It is secular in that marriages must now be registered with authorities to preserve the rights of children born of the marriage. The marriage contract includes elements outlining which partner brings what durable goods to the marriage (for example, carpets, bedroom furniture, living room furniture, and so on).

After signing the marriage contract, the couple is considered "engaged." Engagement is symbolized by wearing a wedding ring on the right hand. During the period between signing the marriage contract and the marriage celebration, the couple may be allowed to get to know one another by going places together publicly. Sexual intercourse is prohibited until the final marriage celebration occurs.

The final step, consummation of the marriage, occurs when all parts of the marriage contract have been fulfilled and the couple is ready to "make house" together. It is celebrated by a wedding party after which the couple may live together as husband and wife. At the wedding celebration, the ring is moved from the right hand to the left, symbolizing completion of the marriage. In some situations, the marriage celebration occurs directly after the signing of the marriage contract. In other cases, it may be several months to a year or more before the final step is undertaken.

Selecting a Partner

So, just how do Egyptians go about establishing a marriage relationship if they are not permitted to get to know one another in a dating relationship? Obviously, if the young people grow up among the group that allows young people considerable freedom in making relationships, the issue becomes more one of choice based on direct knowledge of the prospective partner.

In most cases, selection is by choice, but choice based on little or no direct knowledge of the person's habits or personality. Rather, selection is based on reputation and indirect knowledge. The following is a fairly typical middle-class scenario.

In his mid-thirties, a well-educated and reasonably well-off man I will call Ahmed got increasing pressure from his family to take a wife. He too wanted a wife and family, so began looking for an appropriate mate. Although very sophisticated in manner and dress, Ahmed came from a very traditional family, so had almost no direct interaction with proper, eligible young women from his area of the country. He had several criteria that he wanted in a wife: proper upbringing, educated, preferably pretty, and, most importantly, a virgin. While at a cousin's wedding, he saw a pretty girl, some ten or twelve years younger than he, across the room. They made eye contact and smiled at one another. After the wedding, Ahmed asked friends and relatives about the woman. What was she like? Was she nice? Was she educated? Did she have a good reputation? Upon getting all the right answers to his inquiries, he then arranged to have the marriage contract negotiated. Once the dowry was given and the contract signed, they were engaged. Then the couple took several months getting to know one another to determine if the choice was a good one. "Getting to know one another" meant they were able to go places together in public, such as to a movie or shopping, and to find out if their personalities would work together. Subsequently, the marriage was finalized.

Arranged Marriages

The oldest tradition, that practiced by the more conventional Egyptians, is arranged marriages. Arranged marriages are characterized by little or no choice for the woman and sometimes the man. In all types of marriage arrangements, it is customary for a family member to serve as broker for the marriage contract. Most commonly, the broker is the father. If the father is dead, another male family member, usually an uncle or eldest brother, may serve as broker.

In arranged marriages, the fathers of the prospective couple sometimes negotiate the contract without consulting anyone else. In these cases, the groom may or may not have some influence. The groom's mother also generally maintains significant influence in this realm. The old fashioned way (which still goes on in many sectors of the society) is essentially for the mother of the boy/man to choose her son's wife. Since the man could not really get to know his prospective wife prior to the marriage, he has no basis from which to choose other than recommendations from family or friends. And since women socialize together and know each other's daughters, who is in a better position to make a good recommendation than the man's mother?

Women would get together over coffee or tea to discuss just which girls were available and who would make a good wife. After careful discussion, one would be chosen as the best prospect for the son's wife. Often, the girl would have been brought to meet the future mother-in-law if she were not already known. Most of the time, of course, the girl would be a cousin to the groom and, therefore, the future mother-in-law would already know much about how the girl was reared, including her temperament, reputation, and beauty. Then the marriage contract would be arranged between the fathers.

In some ways, this process could work to the advantage of both partners. A factor that enters the equation is the fact that the man's wife would traditionally come to live in his natal home. She would spend much of her time under fairly direct control from her mother-in-law. It was, therefore, important to have a wife who was congenial not only with her husband, but also with her mother-in-law. And since the couple is not allowed to get to know one another through social interaction, who else knows the young man's behavior and ideas better than his mother? On the other hand, this assumes that the boy's mother wants a good, loving wife for her son. If, to the contrary, the boy's mother was particularly jealous of losing her son's devotion to a wife, she might best choose a wife that was incompatible with her son's personality. By doing this, the mother could assure that her son's devotion was not diluted by the wiles of his new wife. According to people I have talked to, both situations occur.

You almost have to be asking yourself how could the kind of male/female segregation replete with arranged marriages lead to some of the world's oldest, most tantalizingly romantic poetry. I think one of the reasons is because ideas of romantic love were left to the realm of the imagination. If you will notice, much of the love poetry revolves around unrequited love from afar. Usually, the romantic fantasy involves ardor for an imaginary, silk draped maiden or one seen momentarily in the distance. In this poetry, men use flowery language and gestures to win the love of the woman. With these ideas in a man's head, marriage to an unknown woman represents the occasion to wed the fantasy with the real. A woman only known through brief eye conversation, if at all, represents the ultimate in hidden treasures.

For women, the issue is a little different. The possibility of being wooed certainly must enter many girls' minds at some point. However, for most girls, not getting a husband may be a more devastating prospect than marrying someone she doesn't know. Marriage is the only real way to ensure security, shelter and family in the future. Even marriage to a very old man one doesn't know is considered a better option than no marriage at all.

You may now be asking yourself if the girl has a choice about whether she marries the person chosen by her father? Well, sometimes yes and sometimes no. Sometimes a contract between families is arranged when the couple is very young. Some village girls wear an engagement earring even at the age of eight or nine years, indicating their parents have already arranged their marriage. With these types of marriages, the girl has no input or choice. At other times, the girl's mother had input in the negotiation, especially through the selection process mentioned above. The girl can indirectly influence the decision by showing unattractive behavior in front of a prospective mother-in-law, thereby decreasing the chances she will be approved. Among other Egyptians, a girl has the right of refusal and/or selection. Technically, a girl is supposed to have the right of refusal, but this is not always the case in reality. Choice of marriage partners in arranged marriages is, more often than not, a matter of the father's discretion.

Polygamy

Technically, under the laws of Islam, a man may have up to four wives. If a man chooses to have more than one wife, he must treat each of them "equally" in all regards. If he gives one a high dowry, he should give the other/s an equally high dowry. He should spend equal time with each. Polygamy (actually polygyny) is quite rare in Egypt. Most people feel it is wrong for a man to have more than one wife. Most men will also tell you, in a sort of laughing reference, that it is neither financially nor emotionally feasible to have more than one wife.

I have yet to find a woman who likes polygamy. All acknowledge it is legal and acceptable under Islam, but most abhor the idea of being the second wife, much less their husbands taking another wife.

Divorce

An Egyptian man can get a divorce rather easily. Under traditional practices, all he has to do is to state publicly three times in succession, "I divorce thee, I divorce thee, I divorce thee," or words to that effect. If he makes the statement only once or twice, reconciliation remains a possibility. Family members often serve as intermediaries to try to arrange a reconciliation. It is still quite easy for a man to divorce his wife, though the traditional statements must now be accompanied by a legal document filed with authorities.

For a woman, getting a divorce is much more problematic. A woman technically can get a divorce for "just reason," such as impotence or mistreatment. Mistreatment can range from not getting enough food in the husband's household to beatings and so on. Current estimates hold that as many as one in three women have been beaten at least once during their marriage. Only about half of those ever beaten have ever sought help.

The social stigma of divorce is not terribly serious among most Egyptians and the woman's family can usually find her another husband. But some blame does follow the woman if the husband gets the divorce. Sometimes people think she "could have done something to keep the husband she lost." Also, since she is no longer a virgin, her value is less.

Economic factors constitute a more serious reason for families encouraging a woman not to divorce. Family pressures, especially from brothers or fathers, can be substantial. When a woman gets divorced, she then goes back to being the responsibility of her natal family, which means either her father, brother, or uncle re-acquires financial responsibility for her. The family also assumes responsibility to help her get another husband.

Finally, having to leave her children with the husband acts as a deterrent to a woman. In many cases, the children stay with the father after a certain age, usually eight years old for boys and ten years old for girls. The mother might or might not be given the opportunity to see the children again. Most people will tell you that a woman will still see her children occasionally if the husband is a "good person." In spite of the many reasons not to divorce, the Egyptian divorce rate has risen significantly over the past few decades. No specific figures are available, but most people agree that it is more common now than it was in the past.

A 1979 law, which strengthened a Muslim woman's rights to divorce and child custody, was repealed in 1985 after it was found unconstitutional for conflicting with Islamic law. The marriage contract law established in 1931 is now in effect, though a new law introduced in 1995 is pending. If the new law is enacted, it would allow premarital negotiations on a wide range of issues including a woman's right to work, study, and travel abroad. Currently, a woman must have the permission of her husband or father to obtain passports and visas to travel abroad.

Female Genital Mutilation (FGM)

Female genital mutilation (also called female circumcision) still persists in Egypt today. International health organizations widely condemn the practice citing its long-lasting physical and psychological damage. In July 1996, following the death of an eleven year old girl from hemorrhaging, the Minister of Health and Population issued a decree calling for the end of the practice of FGM. Also, the decree called for a prohibition of performing the practice by non-medical and medical practitioners. The exact prevalence of FGM is unclear, but both government and private sources suggest that the practice is common throughout Egypt. It is done to young girls (usually between the ages of seven and ten years old). Best estimates suggest that the procedure is equally prevalent in Coptic and Muslim populations.

Currently, the government broadcasts bulletins condemning the practice. Numerous non-governmental organizations also attempt to curtail the practice by actively trying to educate the population about the hazards attached to FGM. The curriculum at medical schools and for trained birth attendants is being revised to address FGM and its dangers. Finally, the senior Muslim leader in Egypt, the Sheik of Al-Azhar, has stated that FGM is not required under Islamic tenets.

FGM is an intensely ingrained cultural practice that carries with it numerous symbolic traditional reasons for continuing the practice. Many women believe the practice is necessary to ensure that their young daughters will be able to get a good husband and that the practice is a "normal" thing girls must go through as part of growing up. Therefore, in spite of government, religious and private efforts to eradicate FGM, it is unlikely to completely disappear in the near future.

NAMES

Some of the most common names used throughout Egypt give clues on how to fit people into the social structure. You can usually assume that a person with a name common in Islamic history, e.g. Mohamed, is Muslim. People with Western names are more likely Christian. Names that appear in both the *Qur'an* and Bible do not mark a person's religion.

In fact, Mohamed is probably the most common name you will hear throughout Egypt. It is so frequently used that the name is used in conjunction with the next following name or sometimes a person will simply go by their second name to avoid confusion with others named Mohamed.

The use of titles is an important aspect of Egyptian society. The way people are addressed in Egypt is by Mr., Mrs., Madame, Dr., or Professor followed by their first name. For example, a person named Mohamed would be addressed as Mr. Mohamed or Dr. Mohamed as the situation warrants. As a woman, I am sometimes called Mrs. Susan, Dr. Susan, Madame Susan, or Professor Susan depending on the situation and how people know me. Ministerial and high ranking diplomatic officials are referred to as "Excellency." Definitely try to find out any title a person has because to omit their title can be insulting. If you have to err, try to err on the side of giving someone a higher ranking title, rather than a lower one.

A word of caution when meeting married couples. Women do not change their last names when they marry. As a result, it is sometimes difficult to find out a woman's appropriate last name. She may well be introduced to you simply as "Mrs. Fatima, Dr. Mohamed's wife." If you are caught in a rough spot and do not know the woman's name, it is probably better to refer to her as "Mrs. Mohamed" (if that is her husband's first name) rather than to refer to her as "Mrs. 'Husband's Last name.'" This last form of address is usually reserved for informal situations, so should be used only as a last resort in any other setting.

Egyptians are especially proud of being parents. They have a very pleasant, informal way of referring to a person as the "parent" of someone, usually the oldest son or oldest child. For example, a man might be referred to as *"Abu* Mohamed" or "father of Mohamed." A woman could be referred to as *"Umm* Mohamed" or "mother of Mohamed."

People may have many names and recite them differently for different occasions. Don't be surprised if you meet a person under one circumstance and his name is Ahmed Ishmail, only to find that the next time you meet, he is referred to as Ahmed el-Kamel. Usually, sons are named after their grandfather or paternal uncles rather than their father.

DEATH AND INHERITANCE

In Egypt, a person should be buried as soon as possible after death, whether Muslim or Christian. Usually, family members wash the body, wrap it, and then it is interred, often within hours of death. If death occurs at night, it is not necessary to wait until the next day to bury the person as a night burial is appropriate.

A Muslim woman receives half the amount of a male heir's inheritance. By tradition, male Muslim heirs face strong social pressure to provide for all family members who need assistance. A sole male heir receives all of his parents' estate. A sole female heir receives half of her parents' estate with the balance going to designated male relatives.

DRESS

What Egyptians wear and what you will feel comfortable wearing depends to a large extent on where you are and who you are with. In other words, this is another one of those "look around and see what is happening" kinds of topics.

The most visible piece of clothing seen in Egypt is the traditional cotton *galabea (jalabaya)*. A galabea is an ankle length, loose garment worn by men or women. Many of the galabeas sold in tourist areas have short sleeves, but long sleeves are preferred throughout Egypt by most people. Men usually wear white, beige, gray, or light blue galabeas. More prominent men usually wear business suits or casual European or American styled pants or blue jeans with knit or woven fabric shirts (usually collared). Men generally do not wear shorts or tank tops in public unless they happen to be in a tourist area.

Except in the highest fashion areas and around universities, Egyptian women do not usually wear long pants or slacks. Well-to-do women dress in the latest European fashions. For social occasions, prominent Egyptian women wear high heels and expensive (often silk) Western styled dresses and accessorize their dresses with good jewelry – gold or sterling silver, but almost never costume jewelry.

When women think of Middle Eastern clothing, the first thing that comes to mind is the long black cape-like outer garment worn in movies. This is actually seen very little in Egypt except among older women, Bedouins, and among those from exceptionally conservative elements of the population. Short of dressing in a black shroud, what do you wear if you want to blend in most effectively? And, how do you reduce or totally eliminate catcalls, hisses, and propositions as you walk down the street? Essentially, there is no great secret here. Just dress fairly conservatively and direct your wardrobe choices to where you are.

What is least attention getting? Here you can combine comfort with style. It is not necessary to dress in a traditional, brightly colored woman's galabea to fit in. Prominent women dress in Western fashion pretty much everywhere, so this is acceptable as long as you stay within some bounds. Women find wearing long-sleeved, looser fitting garments with all or most of their legs covered to be most comfortable and least likely to attract attention when getting around in Egypt. This can be as simple as placing the blouse on the outside of the waistband rather than on the inside. Short sleeves are certainly acceptable, but probably should cover most of the upper arm. What you will find is that wearing garments with long, loose sleeves (preferably made of cotton or some other natural fiber) is actually cooler in the intensive heat anyway. Loose fitting, natural fiber fabrics form a little air pocket between you and the cloth. Anything made of man-made fibers, such as nylon or polyester, is very hot. When you perspire, man-made fibers tend to stick to you, allowing no air space to evaporate moisture. Cotton underwear is also more comfortable in the heat.

Tight fitting pants are definitely miserably hot no matter what the fabric. For women, almost any kind of long pants (even loose fitting ones) are more appropriately worn with a long, loose over-shirt. Certainly, there is no legal prohibition against tight fitting jeans and low cut or open blouses, but women who wear these demonstrate a lack of respect for local values according to Egyptian perception. Male or female, if you are attending one of the Western universities in Egypt, dress is more typical to that found in North American or British universities. The principal exception is that clothing appears to be somewhat less casual. Jeans are the norm for both men and women in these settings.

Swimwear presents an interesting dichotomy. On normal, every-day beaches frequented by average Egyptians, children and men wear Western styled swimsuits. Women, on the other hand, wear the same thing they do on the streets. And, yes, they do get in the water, long skirts and all, although rarely above their knees. Private beaches are different. Here, depending on who you are with and how private the beach is, the full range of beachwear is possible. Most mature Egyptian women still do not wear Western swimsuits in mixed company on private beaches, but a little more latitude can be found here. Having said that, I will remind you that in tourist areas, particularly on cruise ships or Red Sea villages, you can see anything from bikinis to short-shorts. Western swimsuits of any kind are also all right at swimming pools in hotels and clubs. Most of the time you will find that women's and men's times for access to the pool are

A typical public beach scene in Alexandria. Notice the women's clothes.

separate anyway, so your outfit becomes more a matter of personal preference than propriety.

For men, business meetings and social gatherings require reasonably conservative attire. Here you will find a business suit appropriate for many situations. Alternatively, nice slacks with a dress or sports shirt (with or without a tie) are also acceptable. Egyptian businesswomen dress rather formally, but do not typically wear business suits like the ones worn by women in the United States. They are more likely to wear either a nicely tailored outfit or a dressy dress. Again, natural fibers are preferred since they provide the best protection against the oppressive heat that exists throughout much of the year. Almost always, you will find arms covered. Short, dressy dresses and business clothes have skirts shorter than ankle length, but usually well below the knee.

When in doubt, ask your host or a friend what attire is appropriate for whatever function. There are a couple of important things to remember when asking. First, whenever you ask, "Is such-and-such appropriate," the likely response will be "Yes." You will get this response because your Egyptian friend does not want to insult or contradict you. Therefore, you might get a better answer by asking, "What are you wearing to such-and-such?" or "What will people be wearing to such-and-such?" Second, unless they give you a specific answer, remember that over dressing by your standards is probably preferable to under dressing.

Veiling

The practice of veiling intrigues Westerners beyond belief. Some think it represents the most horrible, archaic subordination women endure in a modern world. Others see veiling as mysterious. Few foreigners view veiling as practical or benefiting women in any way. Western ideas vary about what constitutes veiling in Egypt and throughout the Middle East. So, why do women veil and who veils?

Many scholars believe that veiling was a tradition much older than the *Qur'an*. Apparently, only very wealthy or influential women veiled at the time of the Prophet Mohammed's early life. When the Prophet Mohammed fled from Mecca to Medina (AD 622), some of his followers suggested that his women should be placed in an honored category – so they would be noticeable to all who saw them. Subsequently, veiling became a visible symbol to indicate their difference from others. Wearing the cloak or overgarment also signaled that these women should not be annoyed or given trouble. Later the act of veiling was legitimized in the *Qur'an*. For anyone interested in looking at the reference in the *Qur'an*, see Surah XXXIII, verse 59. You should note that several translations of the *Qur'an* exist. Some translations are more acceptable to Islamic scholars than others. However, this passage does not vary too much from one version to another. Interpretation of how veiling should be implemented in a modern society is a matter disputed throughout the Islamic world. It ranges from the mandated requirements in Saudi Arabia and Iran to personal preference in many other parts of the world.

Stopping to chat, these women are wearing the most commonly seen type of veil.

Not all women in Egypt wear the veil. Veiling can be anything from a large head scarf, pinned under the chin, to a long cloak, head and face covered, allowing only the eyes to show through a slit in the face covering, with gloves and socks. While this type of veiling does occur in Egypt, it is quite rare in the population as a whole. Among the few women who cover themselves completely, color of the veil may vary from black to lavender. Most Egyptian women who veil wear a large head scarf secured under the chin that falls over the shoulders in front and back. This veil may be white or colored. Can you imagine how they could work in the fields covered in a full veil?

Reasons abound for wearing the veil in Egypt. "I wear the veil to show I am a practicing Muslim." "I wear the veil to be inconspicuous." "I am wearing a veil today because I didn't want to fix my hair." "Women wear the veil more now than they did in the past because the economy is not good and women cannot afford to go to the beauty shop as often as they used to."

141

Among the reasons I find most intriguing are the ones relating to being inconspicuous or "becoming invisible." Some of my female students decided to try an experiment to see if they were treated differently when they wore a scarf than when they did not. They found that by wearing a scarf veil they truly could walk among crowds in the most frequented tourist areas and basically become invisible. Wearing the same clothes as before but without a veil, they returned to a popular tourist area with shops, and hawkers and the usual gauntlet of people tried to get their attention. With their heads covered, most of the hassling seemed to disappear.

Chapter Seven

THE EGYPTIAN WAY OF LIFE

HOUSEHOLDS AND HOUSES

Although lifestyles vary considerably by social class and economic conditions, Egyptian tradition fosters extended family ties. It is not uncommon to find three generations of a family living in the same dwelling, whether rural or urban. The best way to look at it is that the more the family can live close together, the better. This means that a family may purchase several flats in the same building, have a villa with separate areas for individual families, live in a village comprised of male relatives with their families, or even live in one flat with separate rooms for individual families. This tradition provides both financial and emotional support for its members.

In urban areas, small, but distinct, areas (called quarters) developed around family groups. New conditions, created by rapid development and increasing urbanization, challenge the ability of many families to maintain traditional living standards. Indeed, crowded conditions in the city also make it harder for urban families to stay together in their family's area of the city. As a result, marriages are delayed until couples can find the financial resources for alternative living arrangements. More and more frequently, marriages cannot be made until the man has sufficient money to get living quarters separate from his family.

When a man marries, his new wife is expected to leave her natal family and move in with his. The distance may not be far, but marriage for a woman meant leaving her familial ties and moving into an established family with which she had no or few ties or history.

Under traditional circumstances, the new bride comes under the control and direction of her mother-in-law who is responsible for the house and household functions. Since the senior woman in the house basically ran the household, daughters-in-law often came under the direct control of their mother-in-law for many aspects of daily living. One may be directed to go to market; another to do the cooking for the family; while a third may do laundry. Certainly, many women were mistreated under this system. Others were treated equitably to maintain household harmony.

For rural people, the challenges are somewhat different. Limited land available for farming means that, in many cases, some males must migrate to the cities for work. In these cases, male workers may be "target" workers or may migrate permanently, establishing new households in the city. Target migratory workers migrate daily, weekly, or for longer periods. In these cases, married workers usually leave their wives and children in the home village, stressing family relationships.

One Egyptian tradition, which crosses all class boundaries, is the habit of adult children living with their parents until they are married. It is quite different from the Western tradition where adult unmarried children establish their own household. One principal exception occurs with migratory male workers. Since more and more rural adult males migrate to the cities to work for wages, increasingly, groups of single males rent flats in the city separate from their families. The same is not true for women – it is still an exception for them to live alone. Young women, even working women, usually live in the home of their parents or close relatives.

Upper-class or elite families have much more flexibility in living arrangements than do others. A family frequently owns villas (houses) and flats (apartments) in several locations throughout Egypt. Apartments or flats tend to be quite different from those in the U.S. or Great Britain. Among the upper-class, flats are often larger than most single family dwellings in the U.S. Family living space is generally quite comfortable. Sometimes a large, family owned villa is divided into flats in which different family groups live. This arrangement facilitates continuation of the tradition of the extended family living in the same quarters. However, in this case individual families have separate flats within the villa. For example, the parents (or widow) may have one floor, a daughter and her family another, and a son and his family still another. Due to recent construction, particularly in and around Cairo, more and more very large buildings house many luxurious flats purchased by the occupants. In these cases, extended family living may encompass a widowed parent living with children and their families or vice versa.

RURAL AND BEDOUIN LIFESTYLES

The *fellahin* (peasant farmers) who typically live in small villages generally practice subsistence level farming and some fishing or work for wages on large farms. Others rent farms from landowners and share profits from farm production. They are often quite poor but more commonly are able to maintain traditional family living patterns. Frequently, a village may be 40 to 50 people all belonging to the same family lineage. For example, one couple may have established the farm a few generations ago, had nine or ten children who, with their spouses, built additional houses, had their families, and so on through the generations.

Fellahin houses look like those that must have been around thousands of years ago. Although electricity is now available in most villages, many houses lack modern toilet facilities, sewage, and piped-in water supplies.

Throughout most of Upper Egypt, village houses are made from earthen bricks (much like adobe bricks in the desert southwest of the United States), sometimes with a mud plaster on the outside. They typically have flat roofs with mud staircases leading to the top. Some maintain areas attached to their houses for animals. Houses typically show little adornment on the outside. Inside walls are often painted with bright colors.

Nubian villages are distinguished from traditional *fellahin* villages by their architecture. Nubian homes tend to be more decoratively painted on the outside than most *fellahin* homes.

Bedouins, who are termed pastoral nomads, typically live in tents constructed of densely woven animal hair. The tent is struck according to prevailing winds to maximize air circulation in the summer

A fellahin house in a rural village – unchanged after thousands of years.

and to protect occupants from blowing sand. In the winter and even on summer evenings, the desert can get quite cold, so tents may be erected close to some type of natural protection, such as in the bend of a *wadi* (dry river or stream bed).

Bedouin groups typically include 40 to 50 persons, usually related. Each family establishes its own small sub-area within the camp. Parents and children have separate sleeping tents. During the daylight hours, children can be seen frolicking around their family's area.

HOSPITALITY

Welcome! Welcome! Everywhere you turn, you will hear this comforting refrain in Egypt. Hospitality is a keyword in Egyptian life. The beginnings of some of the hospitality traditions are unknown, but possibly some began in the desert. People in the desert often offered shelter and food to strangers, assuming that next time they may be the ones in need. No matter where it began, it is now an ingrained tradition everywhere.

Hospitality takes many forms. Some will tell you that by tradition, no matter what the cost to the host, one should provide a guest three days of hospitality. Even if hospitality is not taken to this extreme, you will see some form of typical Egyptian hospitality everywhere you turn. It may take the form of offering you tea in a shop. It may even take the form of sending children to walk with you if you are alone. A common form of hospitality is inviting you to join the family for meals. In cases where you have befriended Egyptians who are not wealthy, use some care when accepting their offers of hospitality too often. They may well spend what, to them, is an exorbitant amount on a meal for you, even if doing so means they would not have money left for other needed things.

Another form hospitality often takes involves being out in a restaurant or cafe. You may well have suggested going to the restaurant or cafe, expecting to pay for all persons. However, when the bill arrives, you may find that your Egyptian host insists on paying for all persons. It would be very embarrassing to your Egyptian friend for you to argue over the bill in public (regardless of whether they can afford the tab). When this happens, wait until you are out of the restaurant and quietly give your friend the money. It is at this point that you can insist without your Egyptian friend losing face. Even so, your Egyptian friend may well tell you that it is "no problem" and that you shouldn't pay. Remember the rule of three's – allow them to refuse your offer twice, but continue to offer until the third time. If they refuse the third time, then it really is all right for you not to pay for the meal.

I find hospitality rules discomforting at times because I am a woman, usually travelling alone, conducting business throughout Egypt. As a result, I run into two factors. First, I am a guest in Egypt, therefore should be shown hospitality. Second, since I am a woman, there is the unwritten rule that men should financially "take care of" women. Therefore, when I try to insist, I often meet resistance even with people I have known a long time. I have figured out that the way to get around this double problem is to insist, and I mean absolutely insist several times if necessary, that they must let me pay because I am on an expense account (whether I am or not). This takes the obligation out of their insistence because I have introduced a third entity, so accepting my hospitality then becomes all right.

FRIENDSHIP

Most Western friendships require little in the form of responsibilities back to the other person – a friend is just someone whose company you enjoy. Being "friends" in Egypt is very different than in the West. Like love, friendship develops rapidly in Egypt. There seem to be few gray areas – people are either friends or strangers. If you are a stranger, you can expect hospitality, but that is all. Once you become a friend, you acquire a complicated web of rights and responsibilities. Friendships require energy and constant nurturing.

Westerners seem to deplore asking friends for "favors." On the other hand, Egyptian friends expect to be able to ask favors of you and expect you to ask favors of them. This is part of the responsibility of friendship. What does this mean in terms of your life in Egypt? Well, if you are not used to having people ask you to do favors for them, a likely response will be to "feel used." You may simply feel imposed upon, but in any event, Egyptian friendships are likely to be considerably more intense than you experience at home. Furthermore, many times a request for a favor may simply take the form of suggesting "I want" or "I would like" to do something, to go somewhere or to have something. Believe it or not, you may be expected to help the person do, go or have whatever it is (assuming it is a reasonable request). At the same time, the slightest hint from you will often provoke a reciprocal action from your Egyptian friends.

Before I was well acquainted with how Egyptian friendships progressed, I was astounded to find that the responsibilities of friendship involved much more giving of one's time and energy than I was used to. One day, I simply mentioned to a friend that I "wanted to go" shopping later that day. I was just making conversation. Certainly, I did not expect my friend to take the comment seriously or as a request for a favor. Next thing I knew, my friend and her children changed all their daily plans to go with me so I wouldn't have to be alone. She assumed that because I said I wanted to go shopping (rather than I was planning to go shopping), that I was expecting her as my friend to accompany me.

VISITING

Visiting friends and relatives is the mainstay of Egyptian social life. Rather than "going" somewhere or "doing" something together as is a common Western custom, Egyptians relish getting together for the sake of being together. Nothing seems to give Egyptians greater pleasure than the company of others. Foreign cultures, on the other hand, often tend toward action. With this action oriented basis for

149

socialization, people often take little time for activities that do not seem to produce some tangible result. Therefore, many foreigners have difficulty with the idea of just "being" with other people. If you are accustomed to getting together with friends to "do" something, "passing by" someone's house for the afternoon or evening to do absolutely nothing but sit around and talk can be unsettling. Furthermore, visits frequently are expected to take several hours. Rarely do visits seem to last just fifteen to twenty minutes (what might be considered to be a polite visit by some standards).

Probably one of the most disconcerting events I experienced passing by someone's house developed when I was invited for the afternoon meal. I duly went for lunch, enjoyed the meal, and settled down for what I thought was going to be a short visit following the meal. After we had chatted for a few minutes, my hosts (who followed the Egyptian custom of napping in the afternoon) offered me a room to take a nap. My initial response was to panic and try to leave immediately. The first time this happened to me, I thought I had overstayed my welcome. I definitely had to fight the urge to run. In retrospect, I realize that they simply wanted me to stay for a longer visit, assumed that I followed their tradition of napping, and were treating me as a family member and valued friend. But to me, without being a house-guest, it was totally unfathomable that I should go to someone's house and take a nap.

DINING ETIQUETTE

Food is definitely part of the Egyptian expression of hospitality and generosity. Now is a good time to think about how you personally perceive food and what is appropriate social eating behavior. Where I was reared, it was impolite to eat a lot when visiting. If this meant you had to eat before you went, OK, but you should certainly not appear gluttonous when in public. On the other hand, not far from where I was reared, the eating in public custom differed radically. Here it was considered bad taste to leave food on the table. In other words, you might have to eat yourself nearly to death, but you must eat all that was prepared or risk insulting your host. These are kind of polar examples, and yours probably falls somewhere in between. I tell you this because certain social rules apply to visiting in Egypt if you want to be a good guest.

First, being a good guest requires you to show appreciation for the food offered to you. How do you do this? By eating. Being a good Egyptian guest is not a one-time, put everything on your plate you expect to eat for the whole meal, event. If you do this, you may find you insult your host when you refuse to take seconds or thirds. You greatly compliment your host by returning for more food, so plan ahead to go back for more food. Refilling your plate once is an almost absolute necessity. Going back twice shows even greater appreciation, but once is certainly enough if you can't possibly hold any more food. More than twice is definitely too much, however. I finally figured out that putting a little food on my plate (for example, by not trying all dishes at once), and spreading the food out a little to make the plate look full, meant I had more room for seconds or thirds. This works particularly well when food is served buffet style.

What happens if your host serves you a food that you absolutely hate and cannot tolerate to even think of eating? In my case, this happens when I face internal organs or seafood. Seafood is easy – I have a medical allergy excuse and this is always understood. But what do you do if you just absolutely deplore the taste of something being served and have no medical excuse? Probably the easiest thing to do in order not to insult your host, is to take just a little of whatever it is you do not want – then kind of move it around with your fork or in some way "pretend" to eat it. Never say something like, "Oh, I'll pass on that – I don't like it."

Taking some of the food offered is especially important if the meal is rather formally served by servants to each individual. In this case, do not pass on a course or dish when it is being served, just deal with it after it is on your plate. Rarely will a servant refuse to remove your plate when the next course is served just because you haven't eaten all of the previous course. Many informal dinners at the home of a friend are served family style. In this case, many of the dishes will be passed around. For other dishes, you will pass your plate for the person closest to the dish to place some on your plate. In this case, you can say something like, "I'll get some of that in a minute, but first I want to try such and such." With luck, they won't notice that you do not ask for some later. Alternatively, of course, just take some. Of course, with buffets, less attention will be drawn to the fact that you simply "skip" a particular item.

I seem to consistently have vegetarians travelling with me. They can run into a particular problem. Many Egyptians do not eat meat with every meal, but do serve it when guests are present as a sign of respect and/or generosity. If you are vegetarian and meat is served to you, again it is probably best to take a little and then just don't eat it. If for some reason you are asked why you are not eating it (highly unlikely), then just indicate that for medical (or religious) reasons you do not eat meat.

If you are the host of Egyptian friends or colleagues, there is one principal rule for good etiquette – never, ever run out of food or appear to be stingy with what you offer! Make many dishes and more than you ever expect to be eaten. If you are having four people for dinner, cook enough of each dish for six or eight. There should always be a lot of food left after the meal. Once, when explaining to a friend about a wedding I attended, I commented that I had never seen so much food at one place in my life. She told me categorically that "there should be as much food left as was eaten after the wedding party was over." This was "to show that you had enough for the occasion." Of course, leftover food will not go to waste. You can always eat some of it the next day. Besides, if you happen to have servants, it is expected that you would offer some of the excess to them.

If you plan to serve food items that essentially are served in one-serving dishes (for example baked potatoes or hamburgers), be sure to have plenty of extras. For example, the concept of the backyard barbecue, where one steak per person is fixed, is totally incomprehensible. "Why," they wonder, "would anyone be so stingy as to fix each person only one piece of meat?" Of course, one of the most important things for a host is to be generous, so having a meal such as this definitely makes you look selfish! Does it mean you cannot have a barbecue? Of course not. It just means you need to cook extra.

MEALS AND FOOD

Except for a few distinctly Egyptian dishes, Egyptian cuisine tends to be a combination of Mediterranean cuisines, typically Turkish, Greek, Palestinian, Lebanese, and Syrian. Egyptians modified ingredients and cooking methods to suit local palettes. While a number of spices are customarily used, they seem to be used in moderation. This gives the food a rather bland taste when compared, for example, to Mexican, Cajun, or Indian food. Added to the standard middle-class diet, you can also find many restaurants that serve sophisticated recipes copied and adapted from Western cuisine.

A typical Egyptian breakfast consists of beans, bean cakes, eggs, and/or pickles, along with bread and *nawashef* or dry things. Hard-boiled eggs (never softboiled), omelets, or fried eggs, onions soaked in vinegar, and mixed pickles usually accompany *fool*. *Nawashef* complements the basic breakfast and includes things like cheeses, jams, and perhaps slices of cake.

'Eish baladi (also spelled *aysh* which is bread), *fool* (also spelled *fuul*, which is boiled fava beans), and *ta'miya* (also called *felafel* or bean cakes) constitute the unofficial staples of the Egyptian diet. The word *'eish* means bread and "life" in Egyptian – "life without *'eish* is not life." *'Eish baladi* is a pita bread, but you can also find *'eish fransawi* or French bread throughout much of Egypt.

There are three main types of broad beans, the basic ingredient in *fool* and *ta'miya. Fool roomy* are large, flat, and whitish; *fool baladi sa'idi*, or local Upper Egyptian broad beans are whitish and middle-

153

sized; *fool hamam* are small, round and dark brown in color. All of these types of beans taste essentially the same, but require different cooking times. When making *fool*, beans are boiled whole for six to nine hours over a slow fire, then mashed with oil, lemon, salt and other flavorings such as crushed garlic, graded onions, chopped tomatoes, and cumin.

Felafel or *ta'miya* is a deep-fried flat disc made from skinned white broad beans. After the beans are soaked overnight, they are drained and minced with dill, coriander, onions, garlic, parsley, leek and other spices. In addition to being delightful by themselves, *ta'miya* are great as sandwiches with either *fool* or *tahina sauce* and salad (chopped lettuce and tomatoes). If you buy these on the street, be sure to tell the vendor whether you want hot peppers added.

Lunch

Lunch is the main meal of the day for most Egyptians. Lunch is served sometime between two and five in the afternoon. Dinner is usually more non-specific. Typically, dinner constitutes eating leftovers from lunch or is similar to the *nawashef* of breakfast. Starches, mainly rice and bread, form the mainstay of the Egyptian lunch and dinner. These are usually wetted with vegetables cooked with meat, chicken, or fish. Lunch and dinner may be accompanied by sweets, which are puddings, desserts, or ices. Beverages served with all meals may be hot or cold. All are non-alcoholic. By the way, most of the time if you ask about a meat dish, the response will be that it is "meat." On many occasions, I have observed people trying to get a more definitive explanation, for example, what animal or what part of the animal. Consistently, the answer is simply "we are having meat."

BAKSHEESH AND TIPPING

Baksheesh and tipping are two entirely separate things to Egyptians although Arabic dictionaries and tourist guide books usually denote them as synonymous. It is especially difficult around tourist areas to distinguish *baksheesh* from tipping. This is compounded by the fact that every local knows the guide books use the words synonymously.

Baksheesh is technically gifts for the poor, a handout, or alms. Beggars of all ages throughout Egypt approach you saying, *"Baksheesh! Baksheesh!"* At first it is very difficult to turn down someone who looks quite helpless and needy – especially if it is a ragged, dirty little child. Very rapidly you will be able to distinguish between the ones that are sent out to hit on any foreigner who appears from others. Let your conscience be your guide regarding giving money, but remember one thing: if you give to one person, you will likely find many others immediately surrounding you asking for money.

Tipping, on the other hand, is considered proper and appropriate for any small service rendered. They have given you something (a service) and you should reciprocate (a tip). Most of the time people are quite courteous if you fail to give them a tip when they deem it appropriate, and simply remind you with a palm up gesture. If they speak your language, they may well remind you with the word "tip" in whatever language. If not, they may use the word *baksheesh* if you seem particularly ignorant to what they expect.

Since tipping is considered rude under some circumstances and simply not necessary in some cultures, foreigners often do not realize that in many situations in Egypt they are expected to give a tip. Furthermore, Americans may find it an affront, especially if the person seems to be doing nothing or is in some kind of uniform. A couple of examples should suffice to show how this works.

First, if you are at an ancient site where there are uniformed guards protecting the place or at an entrance/exit gate, a person from the United States would usually not consider that these people should be tipped. They are employed, getting a salary – just doing their job with seemingly no service provided. After all, they didn't bring you a meal or carry your bag, right? Besides, some are government employees or members of the military. In the United States, it is not only immoral, but illegal, to tip government employees. Why should you tip them?

Well, in Egypt they are performing a service for you – they are protecting you or easing your stay or assisting you in having a good visit. It is true they may get a salary, but like other people in the service industry, their income also depends on getting tips. Their employer is irrelevant. If you look closely, you will see people or tour leaders almost imperceptibly passing a small tip as they shake hands upon going through the gate or when they leave. The average visitor may never notice money exchanging hands.

The same goes for monument watchers or keepers at mosques. These men appear in total silence out of the shadows when you least expect them. They are there to keep disrespectful people from leaving graffiti, trash, or otherwise defacing public monuments. They also tell you in no uncertain terms when you are not supposed to be in an area. Again, you shouldn't make a big deal out of it, just quietly give them a small tip for this service. You will readily differentiate between these men and the ones that appear out of nowhere with goods to sell.

A final example relates to children. Once I was busily taking pictures around Khan el Khalili Bazaar and, since you should always ask people if it is okay, I asked some children if I could take their pictures. All children love to have their picture taken (though women usually don't) and so, of course, they posed. Afterwards, they surrounded me asking for *baksheesh*. A nearby shopkeeper saw them around me and came out yelling at them to leave me alone. I insisted to the shopkeeper that they had given me something (their picture) and I wanted to give them something back. At first, he still did not want me to give them anything because they were "begging," but finally he understood (I think) that it was really only reciprocation on my part.

GIFTS

Gifts are a tough one. Knowing who to give gifts and what to give sometimes seems challenging. Several occasions warrant small gifts. When leaving for Egypt, take small gifts for special people you will meet in Egypt. Gifts should be nice, but need not be terribly expensive.

If you come from a particular region known for a special product, something along these lines would be quite acceptable. For example, I am from Texas, so I usually take along a variety of Texana gifts ranging from coffee-table books to trivets decorated with Texas wildflowers for special occasions. Fine writing pens are always a safe gift for men.

It is also a generally accepted practice to take something to your hostess when being entertained at someone's home. Taking flowers is a custom in many parts of the United States and other Western countries, but probably best avoided in Egypt unless it is something you absolutely know the hostess would like. Unfortunately, until you have been there quite a long time you probably won't know the protocol respecting color, flower variety, or arrangement. You could just as easily go to one of the local flower stands and get a funeral arrangement as a wedding or table arrangement. Sweets, candy, or nuts are a good bet. Most sweet shops will package your gift in a box with a nice ribbon for you to take to your hostess. By the way, do not take something perishable or you run the risk of having it ruin. A proper Egyptian hostess will thank you for the gift and set it aside for opening later (as is the custom with most gifts). If you are hosting and people bring you gifts, you should follow the same practice.

Another category of gifts relates to children. It is acceptable to bring gifts for young children if you know the people well. I like to stock up before leaving home with coloring books, colored marking pens or crayons, and little toys that may not be available in Egypt to give to children of my friends. Be careful not to take anything that has a religious connotation.

A final category of what may be considered gifts are the items you take along to give to people you may meet along the streets or when visiting tourist sites. For some reason, inexpensive writing pens and lighters seem to be premium gifts. Poor children everywhere will often hold out their hands asking you to give them pens. They seem to especially like the ones that click, though any pen can cause furious rivalry within a mob of children. With adults in tourist areas, these small items can often be used as bargaining aids as well as for tips. It is probably best not to take candy or chewing gum for these occasions. Many poorer people do not get their teeth fixed and may have dental cavities, so candy or gum hurt their teeth.

COMPLIMENTS

Complimenting someone on something they have or are wearing can be a little confusing in Egypt. While it is standard practice to tell someone in the United States, for example, that they have a beautiful necklace or ring or anything, you should be a little careful in Egypt. Why? Generosity to a guest is important to maintain a good reputation. As a result, if you are not careful, what is meant to be simply a compliment of good taste places your Egyptian hosts in the awkward position of needing to demonstrate their generosity by offering you the admired object, especially if it is a small, portable object.

The way it works is more or less like this. You can say something like, "Oh, you have a lovely home." People are not likely to try to give you their home. But if you say something like, "This box is so beautiful. I have been looking everywhere for one just like it," watch out. The person you say this to may feel obligated to offer it to you. If you find yourself in an awkward position like this (and it can happen when you least expect it), thank them and refuse. It can get even trickier because they will then try to insist that you take it because they feel they must ensure that you see them as generous. Again, refuse. Usually that will end the offering. A sort of rule of thumb is if something is offered to you the third time, you may assume the person really wants you to have it and is not offering out of social obligation. In this case, you may accept if it seems appropriate to you. You must, naturally, use your own judgement of good taste and propriety depending on the article offered. Just remember that admiration of something will often place your Egyptian friends in the position of having to offer it to you to maintain their social reputation.

One of my most embarrassing moments occurred as a result of window shopping with an American friend along with a friend who was Egyptian. It was close to when I was getting ready to leave Egypt and I did not think about the fact that my Egyptian friend might want to get me a little gift as a going-away present. So as I blithely wandered through some jewelry shops (trying, I thought, to help my Egyptian friend find a token gift to send to someone else), we passed a shop window which had what I considered to be one of the most beautiful rings I had ever seen. So, naturally, I pointed it out to my American friend with a comment like, "Wish I hadn't bought so much, because I would give it all up to have that ring." In my mind, it was so expensive as to be outside the realm of anything for serious contemplation, just one of those nonchalant comments we often make when window shopping. I did not know my American friend was in a small conspiracy with my Egyptian friend. Apparently, all afternoon they had been just waiting for me to comment on some piece of jewelry that I really liked. Had I guessed they might have been looking for something for me, I would certainly have kept my mouth shut about the ring in front of them or would have pointed out something relatively inexpensive as being the absolute thing I most wanted in life. Next thing I knew, my Egyptian friend presented the ring to me over dinner as a gift. The ring is, without a doubt, one of my most treasured possessions that I wear with pride, but you can just imagine my embarrassment when I realized what I had done. I had inadvertently challenged my Egyptian friend's reputation and honor as a generous host.

– Chapter Eight –

BUSINESS

BUSINESS STYLE

People often describe the Egyptian business style as being personal.
This concept interweaves a level of formality into personal relationships built on trust. Who you know definitely carries more weight
than what you know in terms of facilitating business deals in Egypt.
You can always pull in the technical expertise you need, but without
the personal network to make things happen, you are most likely
destined to failure. This is why building personal relationships
becomes so critical to success. The hallmark of Egyptian business
revolves around formality and personal relationships. Formality
typically enters the picture through protocol (who sits where, who is
involved, etc.) and dress. However, personal relationships built on
trust mark the cornerstone of who succeeds and who does not.

Do not be surprised when, upon introduction to an important person, the conversation quickly turns to a "who do you know" kind of scenario. When a person introduces himself at a meeting or someone is introducing you, you will often get a long list of comments like, "I was with so-and-so at such-and-such" or "My cousin so-and-so has been very instrumental in accomplishing this, that, or the other." Do not view this as bragging or name-dropping. That is not the purpose. What the person is doing is letting you know that he has the contacts necessary to fulfil his end of the bargain.

The conversation may follow many forms, but eventually both participants or groups must somehow establish their bona fides in order for the dealings to go forward.

Always, always, always, start business negotiations with the highest ranking person you possibly can. Maneuvering through the system becomes exponentially easier the higher up you start. It is easy to work down a system, but often much more difficult to work up one. However, don't forget the just beginning son of an important businessman, politician, or leader either. Once he is convinced, he may well be able to get his father or uncle interested in your business proposal.

BUSINESS DRESS

Fairly formal is the custom. Remember Egyptians tend to dress a little more formally for most occasions than do Westerners anyway. Dress for men should most often include a jacket and tie, especially for the first meeting. You may find that your Egyptian counterpart is dressed a little more casually during the summer months, but again, it is better to be a bit overdressed than under-dressed. You can always remove your jacket if the situation warrants. Women's dress should either be a conservative dressy sort of dress (not after-five or cocktail type) or a business suit. Definitely do not wear short skirts – the hemline should be at least below the knees.

BUSINESS CARDS

Come armed with lots of business cards! It is customary to exchange cards with people you meet, especially all people attending business meetings. Even if you are not working (male or female), you should have some cards printed to give to people when you meet them.

If you can, have them printed on both sides – one side in English and the other in Arabic. If not, one side in English is acceptable. Many people in Egypt have several phone numbers printed on their cards. Typically these will include home phone numbers as well as e-mail addresses and business and fax numbers. So if you want to impress your Egyptian colleagues with your sincerity and knowledge of customs (and don't mind them calling you at home), get cards printed with your home phone number included. It looks so much better than scrawling the number on the back of the card.

BUSINESS MEETINGS

Two things come to mind when thinking about business meetings in Egypt. The first is time and the other relates to how a meeting is typically conducted. The best recommendation I can offer is practice patience and build flexibility into your schedule.

Some people think Egyptians are chronically late because business meetings never seem to begin "on time" according to foreign practices. This actually is not always true, just a matter of perspective. Whether you arrive at the precise moment your appointment is scheduled, or before, or a few minutes late, you will not be shown into your appointment until host hospitality formalities have been shown. As a general rule, the higher up the official is in an organization or government, the greater the likelihood a subordinate will escort you to a reception room for some time to have coffee, tea, or a cold drink. Of course, as soon as I say that is the standard, an exception occurs. This appears to be a function of perceived rank of the visitor. The more equal in terms of social, political, or business position, the more likely you will be escorted to your appointment and then served refreshments. In any event, Egyptians build hospitality time into appointments and you are expected to adhere to this protocol before business can be discussed.

Egyptians seem to build in a hospitality time in all of their schedules. Depending on the circumstances, some business people actually operate rather punctually, but this is often the exception. Again, you are expected to show up for business meetings on time, however, you will probably find yourself waiting for some time to actually begin the meeting. Even if you are late, do not expect to just walk into the meeting. Most probably, regardless of when you arrive, you will usually be shown to a receiving area and served coffee, tea, or cold drinks, to ensure you are given the hospitality you, as a guest, deserve. I say "most probably" because just about the time you have this all figured out, you will come upon a situation where you are shown directly into your meeting and then served refreshments. This seems to be a practice reserved for some types of situations which are not altogether predictable. The times I have experienced this seem to be when I have had meetings with very highly placed government officials, such as a governor or minister.

Conducting business meetings in your hotel room may be fine in your native country, but you should not do so in Egypt. It is usually best to schedule a separate sitting room for these situations to give the appearance of the seriousness the matter warrants.

As an American, I learned long ago to be a bit sceptical of business dealings with colleagues and to couch business concerns in legalistic, contractual arrangements. In American business transactions, trust goes only so far (and definitely not very far at that). Then one must have the backing of a legal document to bind the commitments. Even when someone gives you their word and shakes on a deal, final negotiations are left to the lawyers. For many kinds of transactions, lawyers may well be required in Egypt as well. Certainly, at some point legal contracts become necessary. However, at a more informal level of negotiation, when an Egyptian tells you on his or her word that something will be done or is agreeable, it becomes a matter of personal honor and the deal will usually be honored. Before you run off to the bank with the deal, however, make sure you actually know what it is you and the other party have agreed on.

An area of common misinterpretation relates to the subtleties of answers given by Egyptians. This is especially true when asking something of a person who considers you a friend (and if you are doing business with them, they probably have put you in the category of friend). As a rule of thumb, when a friend asks you to do something, it is never appropriate (by Egyptian standards) to say no. If an Egyptian answers a request with a noncommittal yes or something like "we must look into this," then the comment actually means "probably no." By the way, this is not to say that Egyptians will not try to get the better of a negotiation – but then, that is all just part of being a good businessman. Does this mean you will never hear "no" uttered in a business negotiation? Probably not, but then it is easy to understand a direct no. The subtleties of the different kinds of "yes" more likely will cause the most misunderstandings.

I have heard Westerners say they were cheated when there was really a misunderstanding as to what was agreed to in the first place. This can lead Westerners to believe that their Egyptian counterparts "lied" to them, when in point of fact they had behaved honorably and honestly according to their own understanding of the agreement. I cannot tell you the number of times when trying to arrange things for my students that I thought there was total understanding as to who was to pay for or arrange what – only to find out later that my counterpart's understanding of the agreement was different from mine. This does not mean that my counterpart acted in a dishonorable or dishonest way – he did not. Rather it meant that we simply did not communicate our respective expectations quite accurately. My only suggestion to avoid this kind of situation is to spell out in minute detail just what you expect. This won't eliminate all misunderstanding, but can certainly reduce the frustration level and number of misunderstandings.

How meetings are conducted requires development of flexibility and patience as well. If you expect to have the undivided attention of your business host during a meeting, you will probably be disappointed or possibly confused.

Frequently, foreigners assume that business meetings will be conducted in a private environment with relatively undivided attention from their business host. Typically during Western business meetings, all calls are stopped or some comment is made to let you know that some terribly important overseas or long-distance call may come in during your visit. You also expect under most circumstances that other individuals either leave or not interrupt the meeting. This is not the tradition for most business meetings in Egypt.

If you are expecting privacy and undivided attention, you may well need to forget this tradition for most meetings. Once you are ushered into your meeting, you may well find you are among five or ten other persons all sitting in the room at various places. Each is also trying to conduct business with the same person. Phones ring and are answered. Long conversations may ensue. People run in and out, catch the host's attention, and conduct their business just as though you were not sitting or standing there. You may find your temper swelling while thinking: "What am I doing here? This person is not taking this seriously. Doesn't this person realize that time is money, and my time is valuable, too?" Actually, conducting meetings in this way is common practice, not a personal statement or action against you.

The times I have experienced exceptions to this type of meeting seem to have occurred most commonly when I have met with ministers or other very high level officials. These individuals seem to follow a more customary Western style business meeting approach, giving you more or less undivided attention. However, it is still not uncommon for a subordinate to come in and interrupt the discussion with pressing issues that simply cannot wait until your meeting is finished.

BUSINESS HOURS

Those accustomed to working from eight to five or, for that matter, seven in the morning to late evening, will find Egyptian business hours difficult to understand. The custom of working for eight hours straight is practically unheard of in most of Egypt. I have alluded to the fact that many shops and *souks* are usually open until late at night. Sometimes these establishments close for some time in the afternoon. Other times they do not close (for example in tourist areas), but you will notice a change in who is working. The reason this happens is the tradition of the afternoon nap.

Bureaucrats do not follow typical Western business hours either. As a rule, bureaucrats seem to work more or less between the hours of nine or ten in the morning through about two in the afternoon. Again, the custom is to leave for lunch around two and follow this with a nap. Usually people are still around the building until a little later in the afternoon, but it seems impossible to get anything done except during the earlier hours.

Of course, if you are working with higher level ministerial people, you may find the hours somewhat different. Some higher ranking officials and other businessmen accustomed to working with Westerners tend to follow a schedule slightly more reminiscent of Western business hours, but do not expect this to be the norm. Count on not doing your work between approximately two and four, with possibly evening meetings as a supplement.

TOPICS TO AVOID

Nearly every book you read gives you hints on topics you should avoid in business meetings or with Egyptians in general. Usually, the well-meaning author reminds you not to ask any in-depth questions about a man's family, particularly his wife or daughters. On the other hand, if you know your colleague has a wife, three daughters, and an ailing mother-in-law, it would seem cold not to make a casual comment roughly stating that you hope all is well with his family (or getting better as in the case of the sick mother-in-law). This shows your friendship and caring for him as a person. Certainly on a first meeting, you should not be the first to bring up the topic of his wife and daughters (most especially if you have never met them). Use good judgement and you probably won't go wrong.

The second topic usually listed to avoid is religion. This can be tricky since many Egyptians may well bring up the subject and you are left trying to figure out how to get out of discussing the topic. And, yes, this can even happen in a business meeting, particularly when you are going through some of the "get-to-know-each-other" protocol. Interestingly, many Egyptians are fascinated about Western Christianity. This is another one of those cases where the media introduces some preconceived notions that might not be accurate from your point of view. For example, some have viewed American televangelists via cable or satellite and assume that all American Christians (maybe even Christians throughout the world) have similar views. Your best bet should you get stuck in an awkward situation is to try to shift the topic around to having them explain Islam to you. That way you can avoid making any statements that could be viewed as hostile or inappropriate, and you are showing an interest in them.

The third topic to avoid is politics, the government or government policy (unless of course you are asking questions about how these things affect your proposed business deal). This is another one of those topics that seem to fascinate Egyptians. Since you are a foreigner of presumed high ranking (or else you wouldn't be there), anything you say may be open to misinterpretation. In a worst case scenario, you could be perceived to be talking for your government. Unless you are a government representative there for that specific purpose (in which case you will have specific instructions), comments on your government's policies or their government's policies could have serious unfortunate repercussions. Egyptians will rarely express a personal opinion about their government or officials that is in any way negative if there are more than two people present (unless, of course, that is their business). They expect you to follow a similar stance.

Discussing sex or telling dirty jokes is not in the best taste either. Once I prepared a briefing sheet for some American university officials and duly reminded them to avoid dirty jokes and discussions of sex. After the meeting (all the participants were men), one of my colleagues quickly came up to me and said, "We didn't know what to do. They started telling us dirty jokes." There are a couple of ways to view this type of behavior. First, your counterparts may well be trying to show you how cosmopolitan they are, thinking that you expect this type of conversation. Second, they may really like dirty jokes. In either event, you may very well lose respect if you start chiming in with, "Have you heard the one about …?" In any event, whether you find the conversation distasteful or just in bad form, not reacting at all or responding with only the very slightest smile will usually get you out of an awkward situation. This is not the place to ask where you can find a prostitute.

NEPOTISM

I hate using the word nepotism – it has such negative connotations in so many countries. Nepotism is defined as favoritism shown to relatives or close friends. Well, in Egypt where so much is based on personal knowledge and trust, logically you find a great deal of favoritism or patronage to family and close friends. It is accepted, expected, and the appropriate way to conduct business affairs. This is how business has been conducted for millennia. You would never consider doing business with someone you don't know or whose reputation cannot be checked through friends and relatives!

No matter how you personally feel about nepotism as a custom, from a pragmatic perspective Egypt's nepotistic practices can work to your benefit in business. Once you have established the trust needed with one person, other doors seem to open magically. It seems that everyone you talk to has a relative doing exactly what you need. Not uncommonly, members of a family will have a brother or cousin or father or uncle or in-law in just the position desperately needed to help with your project.

BRIBES

Only a very fine line of distinction separates bribes from gifts from *baksheesh*. Is a little "tip" given to an official who has helped you get some paper signed a bribe or baksheesh? Depends on your perspective, doesn't it? (See the section on baksheesh for more information.) Some refer to it as the informal cost of doing business in Egypt. Payment of bribes is considered illegal under many foreign laws. In higher level negotiations, certainly direct payment of a cash supplement to an official would seem inappropriate in Egypt as well as elsewhere. It would not, however, seem inappropriate to engage someone (or their son or brother, etc.) who has a separate business (but is also in an influential position) as a consultant or agent on your project.

On a more pragmatic level, sometimes a little baksheesh can assist getting a needed signature in a timely fashion. One situation I observed related to needing a police report for purposes of an insurance claim on goods stolen from a hotel room. The question of retrieving the goods was never a real issue since it was assumed that they were long gone. Rather than calling the police at the time of the alleged theft (which would have involved all kinds of hassles, inquiries and searches), the person was advised that "It would be easier" to wait until later and simply get a police report in another city – cost E£20. Indeed, it took about an hour several weeks later to acquire an appropriate police report for insurance purposes. There was no delay and no hassle and everyone left satisfied (except, of course, for the fact that the goods were still missing).

SETTING UP A BUSINESS

Several types of business organizations exist in Egypt – generally in the form of incorporated companies, partnerships and sole proprietorships. Foreigners are rarely interested in the unincorporated forms used by Egyptian traders.

Most foreign investors choose the Limited Liability Company, known as a WLL (with limited liability). The Joint Stock Company (Shareholder Company) is the most commonly used form of corporate business entity in Egypt. Foreign investors may carry on business in Egypt through a branch office. However, this provides no tax advantage. Companies whose sole interest is the exportation of goods to Egypt must generally appoint a local agent who must be an Egyptian national or company. Labor requirements apply to all companies whose capital exceeds E£50,000.

A good source of information on how to establish a business in Egypt is the National Trade Data Bank, available over the Internet for a fee. Alternatively, check out the American Chamber of Commerce in Egypt website (http://www.amcham.org.eg) for business news.

WORKING WITH THE BUREAUCRACY

Bureaucracies anywhere can be a definite pain! Unfortunately, to establish a business or conduct many business transactions in Egypt requires working with the bureaucratic infrastructure. Rarely can you simply go to the local office, pick up and fill out the papers, and expect things to get done in a timely fashion. It always appears to involve a lengthy process which can try one's patience. True, the Egyptian government is making significant changes to facilitate movement through the bureaucracy, especially for development of new businesses, but reality changes slowly – very, very slowly, no matter how good it looks in the press.

Why is working with the Egyptian bureaucracy so problematic? Of course, part of the problem is the massive paperwork and permits needed to get anything done. But there is one other more perplexing problem. What happened to all those forms you so dutifully submitted to the person at the desk? How could they just disappear into the bottomless chasm of Egyptian bureaucracy? Easy! Everyone must have his input.

Now don't forget that every Egyptian who has a job (especially one of the valued white collar jobs) feels pride and honor with the job. This means they must show how important they are (and that they actually do have a role in the process). Overlaying this need to show personal importance is that old bug-a-boo, deference. Each person must filter every action to the person next in line above them and, no matter what, it seems difficult to jump layers in the deference scale unless – and this is important – unless you have the personal contacts to get straight through to the person you need. This is where having an Egyptian agent (required for some kinds of enterprises) or business partner who is well connected can come in very useful.

Bottom line: getting permissions or permits that should take only pro forma approval may well involve going through many, many lower officials to finally get to the one person who actually has the authority to put the required signature on the needed form.

– *Chapter Nine* –

LOGISTICS

HOUSING

Finding good housing in Egypt depends on what you want and where you want to live. If your company is sending you over, they may have a flat arranged for you. If not, the best thing is to plan to stay in a hotel for a few days or more until you have an opportunity to scope out the landscape. Whether in Cairo or Alexandria metropolitan areas, the first thing you must decide is where you want to live. If you are moving to a smaller city, the options may be more limited than in the two major cities.

Where you want to live will depend principally on your purpose for being there, how long you plan to stay, and what standard of living you prefer. Usually, flats and villas can be rented for a minimum of one month. So, if you plan to be in Egypt for less time, you should count on staying in a hotel or to pay for a month's rent even if you leave before the month is up. If you really want the experience of living in an Egyptian neighborhood, renting a flat or villa is preferable to a hotel. In any event, unless you have some contacts in Egypt prior to going who can arrange your living quarters for you, you will need to stay in a hotel for at least a few days until you can find an appropriate flat.

Housing in Egypt is quite reasonably priced by North American or European standards. The main thing to ask before renting a flat is what is included in the price. I don't mean asking general questions like, "Does this include everything?" If you ask a question like this, misunderstandings are likely to occur. What constitutes "everything" by your standard may be entirely different by Egyptian standards. So, be sure to ask for every specific kind of detail you can possibly imagine. If not, you may find yourself handed another bill for services you thought were included in the rental price. Does it include all utilities – including the phone? If the apartment comes with a phone, how many local calls or minutes are included? Which modern appliances are in the apartment? Is the flat air conditioned (important for summer stays). Who do you contact if something breaks, such as the air conditioner? Is any maid service included?

Another very important feature to consider is how far the flat/villa is from where you work. If you are in Cairo or Alexandria, getting a place to live that is close to where you will be working may be an important consideration. If you have to take taxis around the city all day, you can run up significant expenses on transportation before you know it. On the other hand, if you have a driver or car to move you around the city or live close to a Metro stop, distance from work may be relatively unimportant.

Family considerations also may come into play. Distance from work or usual daily activities may well be less important than having your family close to schools or recreational activities. For example, many Westerners with children prefer to live in the **Maadi** suburb. Maadi is relatively quiet compared to other sections of Cairo. It is a rather upper-class neighborhood of large old homes and gardens. This is a very family-oriented neighborhood where kids can ride bicycles and skateboard. Maadi has great shopping, local churches, a community center, and many other trappings of Western life. The Cairo American College (K-12) is located in Maadi.

Another area you might want to consider is **downtown Cairo** – close to **Tahrir Square**. If you like the noise, traffic, and other trappings of city living, you will love this hub of city life. Activity abounds day and night. Many shopping and entertainment options exist. This area is probably not as good for families with children.

Garden City is quite close to downtown Cairo. It remains an elite residential, diplomatic, and business address. Most of the neighborhood population is Egyptian, however a few foreigners do live here. Goods and services are abundant throughout the neighborhood. Garden City has no private school for English speaking children.

Zamalak has some of the best shopping and restaurants in Cairo. It is located on the northern end of **Gezira Island** and is home to the famous Gezira Sporting Club, public green areas, and a new public library (the Greater Cairo Library). The British International School is located in Zamalak.

All in all, living in Egypt can be relatively inexpensive, but the cost can rise rapidly depending on the choices you make. Prices can range from absurdly low to very high, depending on what you want.

LAUNDRY

Forget laundromats – they don't exist in Egypt. On the other hand, getting your laundry done in Egypt is usually quite easy and relatively inexpensive. All major hotels have laundry service available. As a local resident you can get laundry services (known as *makwagis*) in all neighborhoods around Cairo. Other than doing laundry yourself, sending clothes to a makwagi is the traditional method. Things to remember when sending your laundry out are to communicate exactly what you want done and make a list of what you send. These days, clothes are sometimes drycleaned instead of laundered – even underwear. So, be sure to check! If you do not want clothes washed in hot water, tell them. If you do not want bleach added, tell them. If you want clothes drycleaned, tell them. Most clothes will come back ironed, so if you do not want clothes ironed, again, tell them. If you do not state precisely what you want, you may be surprised with the results. Unless you have someone that you know hand washes clothes, do delicate items by hand at home. If you have a family or expect substantial laundry needs, consider purchasing a washing machine after you get to Egypt. A washing machine will cost about E£2,000, but you can probably sell it when you get ready to leave.

MEDICAL CARE

Especially in the major cities, access to fairly good general health care services is readily available. However, you should do some pre-planning to ensure you won't have to take whatever you can find in an emergency or when someone gets sick. Like almost everything else in Egypt, medical care facilities run the gamut from little or nothing to a few hospitals equipped with the most modern technology.

Just as in a move to any other new city, it may be best for you to make contact with a physician upon arrival to find someone you like and can trust. For example, many well-trained and knowledgeable specialized physicians are professors at the University of Cairo Kasr el-Aini Medical School. These physicians typically also have a private practice office (called a surgery or clinic) where they see patients at various hours of the day. This is not eight to five medicine. Physicians may see patients at their clinics at all hours of the day and night, depending on their personal schedule. Make sure to find out when your doctor sees patients, how to contact him/her at all hours, and what you need to do to make an appointment. Also, find out at which hospitals the physician sees patients. This may make a difference in choosing a physician for a long-term relationship. Surprise of all surprises, many Egyptian doctors will come to your home or hotel to see you.

Generally speaking, Egyptian physicians practice a more humanistic type of medicine than most Western physicians. This means that they listen to your symptoms, may palpitate as needed, but rarely utilize extensive laboratory measures for most common ailments. They do not have a queuing system such as occurs in Great Britain and in some managed care programs in the United States. What this means in practical terms is that if what you need is available and you have the money to pay for it, you can reasonably expect to be able to get the service you need.

It is advisable to discover the locations of hospitals in a new place. In the event you might need one, it seems best to know approximately where it is located in the city and which one you would want to go to. Numerous "private" hospitals exist in and around Cairo and Alexandria. Designation as a private hospital may be somewhat different than you are used to in your own country. A number of these small private hospitals are owned by one or more physicians. Just because a hospital is called a private facility, it does not mean that it will be a big, technologically sophisticated facility. Most small private hospitals are essentially open-air medical facilities. That is, they do not have sophisticated, recirculating air heating and/or cooling units with closed, sterilized wards or rooms. Instead, most small hospitals are built more on the traditional Egyptian pattern with open doors and open windows throughout. Most commonly, small Egyptian private hospitals are equipped to handle general medical problems, with only somewhat limited access to surgical procedures or physical therapy. Only a few major hospitals are built on the Western model and equipped with modern technology.

It will probably be in your best interest to make sure any specialized health services you will need on a maintenance basis are available before going to Egypt. For example, if you are going to need allergy injections on a regular basis, you may want to bring the vaccine with you to cover the time you expect to be in Egypt. In this case, you might also want to be sure to purchase a disposable syringe at a local pharmacy, just in case the doctor you go to only has reusable syringes. Similar precautions should be taken for situations such as diabetes.

Unless you are coming from a cholera prevalent area, no immunizations are required to get into Egypt. However, some potentially life-threatening diseases occur often enough in Egypt to warrant consideration of immunization prior to arrival. Immunizations to consider include: Viral Hepatitis A (HAVRIX); Hepatitis B; Typhoid; Poliomyelitis; and Tetanus/diphtheria. A final issue to discuss with your physician is a pre-exposure rabies vaccine. Anyone having the pre-exposure rabies vaccination series will still have to undergo post-rabies treatment, but the treatment is milder than for someone who has not had the pre-exposure vaccine.

The Center for Disease Control (CDC) in Atlanta, Georgia, has immunization recommendations for travel to Egypt. The latest assessment from the CDC can be accessed on the Internet at: http://www.cdc.gov/travel/. Similar programs and recommendations exist through major public health entities or from your government in most countries throughout Europe. Check with your physician before leaving for Egypt to ensure that you have all recommended immunizations.

Pharmacies

Small pharmacies are located throughout Egypt. Many medications that require a doctor's prescription in North America or Europe can be bought over the counter in Egypt. To purchase narcotics, you will need a prescription from an Egyptian physician.

If you know you will be needing a specific, very specialized medication during your residence in Egypt, best to bring a supply with you. Make sure to keep any prescription medication in its original container with the label attached to avoid any possible confusion at customs. It is usually recommended that you also bring a copy of the physician's prescription with you.

Most commonly used medications, though definitely not all, are available in some form in Egypt. However, pharmacies may run out of the very thing you need or may have drugs commonly used for an ailment, but not the one you want. Also a particular medicine may be available in a syrup instead of a pill, or vice versa, but available. For example, I once desperately needed a specific kind of asthma inhaler. The pharmacist had inhalers, but none with the specific composition I needed. Another time, I needed an expectorant cough medicine and was able only to find a cough suppressant medication. In this case, I did not know a chemical name I needed, so the pharmacist kept bringing me the wrong medicine.

It is best to know what medicine you want to buy when you go to the pharmacist. But even if you do not know what medicine you need, the pharmacist will gladly recommend medication based on what you tell him/her you need it for. If you do know what medicine you want to buy, such as a type of antibiotic, be prepared to give the pharmacist the generic or chemical name of the medication. Do not count on being able to find the brand named drug sold in your country of residence. Also, quality control problems in the Egyptian pharmaceutical industry occasionally occur. Those who use contraceptives should bring their own brand since local pills may cause side effects.

Optical Supplies

If you wear glasses or contact lenses, you will be significantly more comfortable if you bring spares with you to Egypt – just in case you break or lose them. At the very least, bring a copy of your lens prescription with you. Egyptian optical shops are sometimes difficult to find and often have erratic hours, but you can get both single and bifocal lenses replaced. Small repairs are relatively inexpensive and most optical shops can accommodate you.

When you try getting something like glasses replaced, remember that it probably means you will be operating on Egyptian time. So, if you should break your glasses and actually need them to function, you could be out of luck for some time. The alternative, of course, is to have someone from your home mail you a spare pair. This can be quite expensive, but you could probably get them faster than having a new pair made in Egypt. Never trust the regular mail with something like this, but use one of the express mail carriers. The same applies to prescription sunglasses. Good sunglasses are definitely a necessity to combat the glaring sun and blowing sand. You can find good sunglasses in Egypt, but they might be expensive.

If you wear contact lenses, take special precautions. You may experience discomfort wearing contact lenses in Egypt's arid environment. Add air pollution and blowing sand, and contact lenses rapidly become painful and in need of replacement. Even if you have worn contact lenses for years, you should bring a backup pair of glasses for those days when your eyes are irritated by the environment. Many people have found that they cannot wear contact lenses at all in this environment.

Also be sure to bring any specialized cleaning equipment for contact lenses with you. Contact lens supplies such as sterilized wetting solutions can be found fairly easily, but as in the case of prescription drugs, specific brand names may not be available, so any specialized formulas you require should be brought with you.

Baby Supplies

Baby formulas, such as Similac, SMA, and Nestle are available in powdered form in Egyptian pharmacies. You can also find items like cough syrups for infants and Vap-o-rub.

Things you should bring with you if you have small children include training pants, receiving blankets, crib sheets, a blender for preparing baby food, a play pen, door gate, extra baby shoes (at least one size ahead), car seat or stroller, baby thermometer, diapers and rubber or plastic pants. Disposable diapers are available, but they are very expensive.

Toiletries

You can find most types of toiletries and cosmetics in Cairo and Alexandria (but not necessarily in the smaller cities). They may or may not be the brand you are used to. If you prefer specific brands of, for example, antiperspirant, cosmetics, or shampoo, bring them with you or take a chance of having to use another brand. You should also bring bug repellent and sunscreen lotion with you if you require anything above SPF15.

Even when I go for short visits, I always take a small first-aid kit with me. You can buy these ready packaged or make one yourself. Don't forget bandages, individually wrapped alcohol swabs, and especially an antibacterial cream. If you have very sensitive skin, take a tube or two of some type of cortisone ointment for those pesky itches. Special skin cleansing supplies for acne should be brought with you. Some other items you may wish to bring are hair curlers, tampons (very expensive where available – a box of 30 costs about E£30), panty liners, and hair dyes along with anything you need to go with them if you want to maintain comparable tints.

Special Foods

Before you leave, take stock of what particular processed things you really can't live without. For instance, one of the things I must have is Picante Sauce, which is not available in Egypt. On the other hand, all the things you need to make a really good salsa are there, so if you don't have to have the store-bought kind, you will do fine. A lot of foreign products are not likely to be found in Egypt. One of the things to consider stocking up on before you come are those handy little packets of sauce and seasoning mixes. Special ingredients for Mexican foods are not available, so bring your favorite chili mix.

Other things you cannot find (at the time of writing) include decaffeinated coffee and tea. Diet sodas are available, but often hard to find. The same goes for salt substitutes. There is one type of artificial sweetener but individual packets of that are rarely available in restaurants. If you are addicted to Koolaid, Gatorade, and Crystal Light, try changing your taste to a local drink mix. Instant coffees are stocked, but individual bags for brewing a cup of coffee are not. If you must have brown sugar, maple or corn syrup, shortening, chocolate chips, cream of tartar, pecans, and mincemeat – bring them with you. Don't forget your favorite cookbook!

KITCHEN AND HOUSEHOLD SUPPLIES

Bring whatever favorite kitchen utensils you think will make you feel at home. There is nothing worse than not having your favorite things in the kitchen – especially if you have to cook every day. Many flats will come with minimal kitchen supplies and you can always supplement these in Egypt, but it may be quite costly since most will be imported (therefore, highly taxed). Small kitchen appliances are available, but more expensive than if you brought your own. Consider packing all your own small appliances, such as toaster ovens, toasters, coffee grinders, coffee pots, microwave oven, mixer, food processor, blender, etc.

Bring power strips. If you do this, then you will only need to buy a voltage transformer. You can buy one in Cairo for less than you would pay for any of the appliances listed (about E£170 for 500 watt, E£300 for 1000 watt).

Some people prefer to purchase everything in Egypt – use your judgment based on your budget and length of stay. Remember, if you import appliances under temporary admission in your air freight, you must take them out of Egypt at the end of your stay even if they no longer work. So don't throw away those broken appliances if you import them this way.

Bring lots and lots of plastic storage bags, ties, and sandwich bags. Zip-lock bags are not available and can win you many points as gifts to friends. Measuring spoons and cups here are not in cups or ounces. Absolute musts for any cook that you need to bring include a kitchen timer, rubber spatulas, corkscrew, your favorite knives, cookie sheets and special cookie cutters, canisters, a large plastic tablecloth, hotpads, potato masher or pastry cutter, and anything else you use consistently.

Paper napkins, paper towels, waxed paper, aluminum foil, linens, utensils, and tableware are available at local markets. Pesticides and cleaning supplies are also available

ELECTRIC CURRENT AND EQUIPMENT

Certain adaptations are required for using American appliances in Egypt. Things to consider include voltage, cycles of alternating current, plugs and wall sockets, wattage, and power surges. To use American appliances, you must have adapters, voltage converters, transformers, and voltage regulators. If you plan to bring small American appliances to Egypt, you will need to know the following.

Egyptian current ranges between 220 and 240 volts (but can drop to well below 200) alternating at 50 cycles per second. Egypt's voltage can be brought down to 110–120 by using converters (for small appliances) and transformers (for large appliances). Voltage converters come in two sizes: one for appliances using up to 50 watts, and another for appliances using 50–1600 watts. Converters do not work on appliances over 1600 watts.

Egyptian outlets are the "Continental" type, requiring plugs with two round prongs. These are different from British plugs that have two slightly shorter, slightly fatter, round prongs.

The difference between 50 and 60 cycles is not significant for most equipment – most simply run more slowly. Cyclical differences cause a problem with items that use alternating currents to produce a given speed of operation, e.g. clocks. Some modern appliances operate on direct current, thus have no problem. Others can operate on either 50 or 60 cycles. Check your appliances before bringing them to find out if they will work at 50 cycles.

Since Egyptian current varies between 200 and 240 volts, voltage regulators/stabilizers should be used to convert an uneven voltage input to a rather steady output. Voltage regulators/transformers are available in Egypt. These will also convert 220 volt current to 110 volt current.

A special note for those bringing computers. Prior to leaving, determine what you will need to operate your computer on 220 volts 50 cycles. Usually you will need a transformer to convert the current to 110/120 volts 50 cycles. A voltage regulator is definitely a necessity to protect the computer from current fluctuations. Bring diskettes (expensive in Egypt) and boxes for the diskettes (can't be found in Egypt).

Fax machines are quite heavily taxed. When bringing one into the country whether by accompanied baggage or air freight, it will be kept at the airport until clearance from the Ministry of Communications has been granted and until you have paid an import fee of E£600 to the Ministry. Then you must pay an annual usage fee of E£500 (this will be on your telephone bill). Fax modems are a different issue. There is no fee charged for a fax modem, but it should be listed on your inventory as a "computing accessory" to avoid confusion.

TVs, Radios, and VCRs

U.S. made TVs (NTSC system) will not work in Egypt (which uses the PAL-SECAM system), but you can purchase color or black and white sets in Egypt. VCRs are available in Egypt that adjust to all three systems, but they are expensive. You will need a shortwave radio receiver if you wish to get Voice of America or BBC radio.

MONEY AND BANKS

Most private transactions in Egypt seem to be by cash or credit card. The good news is, banks are seemingly everywhere in Egypt. Furthermore, in some of the larger hotels, you can find them open most hours of the day. Banks typically close on Fridays and often for several hours during the afternoon. Some exceptions to this rule are the banks located in major hotels, which may operate special hours due to the high tourist traffic.

Exchanging foreign currency or cashing major brand traveler's checks is rarely a problem. You will need your passport to exchange money or cash traveler's checks. ATM machines are now located in many of the larger hotels, so in an emergency (and assuming the system is working at both your home bank and in Egypt) it is possible to directly get funds from an account at your home bank. For long term residents, establishing a bank account at one of the larger international banks located in Egypt is probably easiest. Cashing foreign checks, other than traveler's checks, can involve a quite lengthy procedure often taking several weeks before you can get the money.

Internationally recognized credit cards, such as American Express, Visa, and MasterCard, are accepted in many places throughout Egypt. Some places that accept credit cards have different rates for credit cards and cash. When you plan to make a purchase, it is best to ask in advance if there is a difference in cost. Small shops, local services, local businesses, and of course the multitude of private vendors on the street do not accept credit cards. For these you will need cash. When in doubt, just ask.

COMMUNICATION

Mail Services

The Central Post Office in Cairo, located in Midan el-Ataba, is open 24 hours a day. All other post offices are open from 8:30 a.m. until 3:00 p.m. every day except Friday. Most major hotels have outgoing mail boxes. Stamps are available at most hotels.

There are several ways to send packages overseas. An export certificate must first be obtained at the Central Post Office. Usually, the store from which an item was bought will take care of these formalities for you, for a small fee. Several express mail carriers also have offices in Cairo. They are expensive, but will also take care of all formalities.

Phones

Egypt's telephone system has improved considerably in the past few years, but is still far from perfect. Public phone booths may be found around stations, in main squares and hotel lobbies. Some store owners may permit limited calls to be made from their lines, but you should always offer to reimburse them for the service. Telephone offices also have a large number of phone booths for both local and overseas calls. There you can purchase phone cards that allow you to talk until the amount of the card is used. In public telephone offices, numbers are assigned and called out for you to pick up the line when the connection is made.

Major hotels are another excellent place to make overseas calls. Most of the better hotels have telephone services that can connect you directly to major international telephone company operators such as AT&T or MCI. If you have a calling card from the company, your call will be charged directly to your bill. Otherwise, you may pay directly to the phone service at the hotel. In any case, there will be a small charge for using the hotel service. Most international telephone companies also now allow collect calls to be placed from Egypt. Collect calls cannot be made from Egypt except through these international companies.

Many rented flats and houses come with telephone lines installed. If your flat does not have phone lines installed, it can take some time to get one without a rather large payment for immediate service. Even on home phones, calls are charged by the time used, not a flat user service rate.

Faxes and the Internet

Commercial fax service is widely available throughout Egypt at business centers located in most "better" hotels. Internet services are increasingly available in Egypt, but as of 1997, personal service was still somewhat limited. As of this writing, several companies offer Internet connections for a rate of approximately 1,100 to 1,200

Egyptian pounds per year. Late in 1996, two Internet cafes opened in Cairo, one in Garden City and one in Maadi, where hourly access is available for a reasonable fee. Additional walk-in Internet services are scheduled to open in Alexandria and Cairo. As access to the Internet becomes more available, services should develop in other cities. Check with major hotels for any new services available to customers through their business centers.

PETS

From all accounts, taking a pet to Egypt presents no major problems. Be sure to consult the airlines and a veterinarian about carrying cases, etc. The Prevention of Cruelty Society and some airlines offer pamphlets about preparing your animal for a long journey. Any animal brought in must have a veterinarian's certificate on the veterinarian's letterhead indicating the animal is healthy and has had an anti-rabies vaccination. This document must be certified by the authority under which the veterinarian operates. The pet must be examined within 14 days of departure. Even with this document, Egyptian agricultural officials may, if they see fit, hold the pet in quarantine for up to 15 days at a cost of E£1.50 per day, excluding food. All expenses for the animal must be borne by the pet owner. You should try to make arrangements through company officials in Egypt, a friend, or your travel agent to make sure the Egyptian Veterinary Department at Cairo Airport is alerted to the fact that you will be entering the country with a pet. There will be a minimal entry tax for dogs. Once this is paid, the animal will be issued an identity tag which should be attached to the collar for easy identification. Cairo has a well-equipped, excellent veterinary hospital, should one be needed.

Of more concern is repatriating the animal upon leaving Egypt. For the U.S., this is no problem. Again, it requires health and vaccination certificates. For the U.K., animals are currently required to be placed in quarantine for a period of six months when they enter the country. The best thing to do if you are planning to take an animal is to check with the nearest Egyptian Consulate as well as with your local government authorities to check any restrictions that may be imposed.

Boarding facilities for pets are extremely limited in Egypt. So if you plan to travel within Egypt, you should consider that you will have to get a petsitter or neighbor to look after your pet while you are gone. Imported pet food is available, but expensive, so many people make their own pet food. You can add vitamins and mineral supplements that you bring with you. No prescription pet foods are available in Egypt.

Pets cannot run free due to the large number of loose animals with diseases. Rabies is fairly prevalent among the stray cats and dogs around Egypt. Given this, you might want to consider bringing baby gates for doors so you can keep the animal contained easily within a small space in your residence.

Many Egyptians do not like dogs. Some of this feeling relates to traditional roles of dogs and the number of strays running around loose in the cities (mentioned in Chapter Three). In addition, those with conservative interpretations of Islamic tradition tend to regard dogs as dirty. These people, especially, do not want to touch or be touched by a dog. Make sure anyone you hire knows there is a pet in residence and what rules apply regarding the pet's treatment. Unless you know a person likes dogs (and yours in particular), it is best to seclude the animal when friends come over. This is also something to keep in mind when hiring people to work in your home. That way, no one is insulted or uncomfortable.

SERVANTS AND SERVICE PEOPLE

If you have never been able to afford a maid or a cook, this may be your chance. One good way to find a reliable and honest household servant is to ask among friends that already employ someone. You will likely find that whoever works for your friend will have a relative or friend that is just what you want. If your friend's employee is a good person, they are unlikely to suggest anyone of lesser character because to do so would look bad for them.

Once you have found the perfect person/s to work in your household, several etiquette factors come into play. People who have never had servants may actually find the situation uncomfortable. How do you treat a servant? Preconceived notions abound, from treating them like one of the family, to treating them "equally" to anyone else who enters the household, to talking down to your servant. Certainly, there is no need to talk down to a servant, either in private or in the presence of guests. To do so in front of guests would make you and them lose face, and cause you to lose the respect of your Egyptian friends. You can also count on any mistreatment on your part getting around through the local grapevine.

What if you are more inclined to treat your servant as a member of the family? Or, what if you have sincere notions about equality and are afraid any act that treats the servant differently implies unfairness? Well, there is definitely a middle ground that is appropriate in Egyptian society. The basic rule of thumb goes something like this: private and public behaviors are different.

You may well develop a warm and personal relationship with your employee, often sharing jokes and laughter together. In fact, it is quite appropriate for you to develop a feeling of responsibility, much like a family member would do. This includes being very generous with your employee, especially with things like surplus food, and clothing or other items you no longer need. Because they feel you are like family too, you may find them asking you for help with medical expenses or in a family emergency. This is normal and expected behavior – it does not mean they are trying to take advantage of you. As their employer, you are in some ways responsible for them just as if they were members of your family. If you feel you cannot afford to give them all that they need or feel it is too much, at least give them something to show your concern for their well being. Not to do so would be an insult. If you are concerned that the amount requested is too much, ask your friends to see what would be appropriate. Then, if need be, you can arrange to take some of it out of your servant's wages in the future.

This is the private side of your relationship with your servant. It is reserved for when outsiders are not around. When outsiders are around, especially other Egyptians, behavior changes. In these situations, your servant should be accorded the opportunity to show others how well they do their job and provide a service to you. For you to do any work in front of others that should be their job will embarrass them and your Egyptian guests. It is a matter of pride and respect for them to want to do all the work by themselves if others are present. For example, you and your cook may well have worked together making table arrangements or preparing the meal for a dinner party. This is all well and good. But when the guests arrive, you should not be seen doing any of the work. If you do, it implies that your server or cook is incapable of doing the job for which they were hired. It also shows you do not know how to behave properly.

Never hesitate to say please or thank you when the situation warrants. Just like anyone else, servants appreciate the simple courtesies and actually expect to be treated with this type of respect by Westerners.

Making friends with shopkeepers, taxi drivers, and other people you meet in your daily activities can provide one of the greatest ways to get to know about Egypt and Egyptian life. Don't be surprised if you are quickly invited for a dinner or to make social visits. In these cases, you should remember that they may not really be able to afford your company – to be able to receive you properly. Go, but remember that frequent social visits place a financial hardship on the family. Since you may find you really enjoy the friendly company of someone who can't afford your visits and you would like to continue the relationship, take gifts or find some other way to compensate your host. You could do something as simple as asking them to do some little job for you so you could make sure they had extra money. For women, you might suggest that the wife give you cooking lessons or teach you how to go to market properly. You could always buy enough cooking ingredients for two families and share this with them. Or, you could buy them something in which they showed a special interest. Any little thing like this would give you the opportunity to give important, needed gifts and not take advantage of your friend's hospitality.

Once some friends of mine were going out of their way spending money to be with me and my group that I knew they couldn't afford. I tried all sorts of ways to try to help with the financial responsibility I knew they could ill afford. I arranged for them to have a special dinner and cake for their anniversary. I took presents to their daughter – things that I knew might be outside their budget, but wanted or needed. Once, when the wife was taking us to the beach and had forgotten her sandals, I gave her mine, insisting I had another pair upstairs. Use your imagination and you can come up with all sorts of ways to relieve them from the financial burden of their culture's generosity without insulting their hospitality. When I left the country, I had all sorts of clothes, toiletries, and things that I insisted she take – either for herself or to give to someone she thought might need or want them.

MISCELLANEOUS NECESSITIES

Things that drive me crazy are bathroom things I don't have or can't find. There never seem to be drain plugs that fit anywhere. Bring several of the wide, flat ones (rubber deteriorates very quickly in Egypt). In an emergency, I have actually used plastic bags, but this is definitely not the long range solution! Another handy thing to have around is a small household tool kit. Include things like picture hangers, hammer, small nails, etc.

Sometimes it gets pretty cold and a sleeping bag is a lifesaver during winter months. It is also handy for overnight trips to the desert. Remember, many places are not heated and it can definitely get quite cold during winter nights. I have been known to sleep under blankets,

in a sleeping bag, while wearing a sweat suit and long socks on the coldest nights. This makes it tolerable, but not necessarily cozy.

I think a small daypack is an absolute necessity for each person (except small babies, of course). The kind that is most comfortable has a foam rubber pad directly next to your back. I put little combination locks on zippered waist pouches and backpacks to insure that anyone trying to get stuff out of them has to cut them or slash them off me. At least, I am more likely to know it has happened than if they just have to unzip the bag. While I am thinking about it, in a crowd, wear your backpack on the front. This also cuts down on any untoward actions. Other miscellaneous items to bring with you include: clothes pins, sewing notions, velcro, bathtub mat, skirt hangers, mattress pads (can't buy them in Egypt), a travel iron, non-disposable flashlight, special holiday things, sheet music if you are a musician, extra guitar strings, etc., and hobby supplies. Definitely don't forget your children's favorite games and toys! Some Fisher-Price and Lego toys and games are available in Egypt. Bring pictures to hang on the walls. Nothing can be more depressing than bare walls or nothing to remind you of home.

Chapter Ten

ENTERTAINMENT

CULTURAL ACTIVITIES

Lots of cultural activities exist in and around Egypt. You can choose from theater, dance, opera, symphony, and cinema (foreign and domestic). The Cairo Symphony performs weekly during the winter months at the Cairo Opera House. Also, performances are staged at the Opera House by visiting companies from Europe and the United States.

Foreign and local cultural centers offer a variety of options. They offer activities such as language classes, films, exhibits, and recitals. In Cairo, some of the more active are the British Council, the Goethe Institute, and the American, Austrian, Canadian, French, Italian, Japanese, and Spanish cultural centers. In Alexandria, check out the American, British, French, German, Italian, Russian, and Spanish cultural centers.

Among the other options in Cairo are the American Research Center in Egypt's (ARCE) Archaeology Club, which offers field trips and a series of lectures. If you are interested in drama, the Maadi

Community Players is an option. Several Christian churches and religious groups around Cairo offer religious and social programs. Among these are representatives of the Anglican, Protestant, Catholic, Christian Science, Quaker, and Mormon groups.

There are also several women's groups that generally welcome new members and especially those with interests they would like to share. Women should check on the Maadi Women's Guild. This group arranges get-togethers and lectures, and offers opportunities for volunteers to help several Egyptian charities. The Women's Associate of Cairo also offers many opportunities. The Community Services Association is a gem, offering lots of classes on a large variety of subjects.

Cinemas

Egypt's cinemas are relatively inexpensive by Western standards, with tickets most commonly ranging from E£4.5 to E£10, except during the International Film Festival.

Libraries and Bookstores

If you are addicted to reading and need a new novel a week to keep you going, bring a good supply with you. It will be cheaper and significantly easier. Public libraries do exist in Egypt, for example the new library in the Zamalak neighborhood of Cairo (the Greater Cairo Library). Plans are also under way to open the new Alexandria Library in 1999. Many Egyptian libraries are affiliated with universities, schools, or private associations. Even if you are allowed access, you may not find the variety of materials you are accustomed to in your home country's libraries, especially in the way of fiction. Some universities allow the general public to use their resources as reference materials, but do not allow individuals to check materials out from the library. The American University in Cairo (located at Midan Tahrir) has one of the better libraries and their bookstore is a treasure trove. The library is down the street and across from the main entrance to the University. You will need to check with the University regarding access to the library and hours of operation. Also, check with the various embassies to determine what resources they may have available to the public. Other than that, a few small private libraries exist, but access to them is generally quite limited and very hard to find.

On the other hand, numerous bookstores exist throughout Egypt. Most, quite naturally, carry predominantly Arabic publications. However, several carry rather extensive selections in English, French, and German. Bookstores range from small, hole-in-the-wall places that are musty, dusty, and confusing, to well-arranged, spacious stores with staff members that seemingly know every book in the place. You will not find the huge, mega-selection discount bookstores typical of the United States and Europe anywhere in Egypt. Some books are simply not available in Egypt. Relatively speaking, books of any type are actually quite expensive in Egypt. An event to look for is the International Book Market that occurs in early winter in Heliopolis.

Almost all major hotels have kiosks that carry a limited selection of English, French, and German reading materials, including some fiction. Typically, their selections may include a few best seller selections, one or two classics, and perhaps some biographies. Mostly, hotel kiosks carry coffee-table books, tourist books, and publications related to Egyptian antiquities since tourists represent their principal market.

Definitely check out the Community Services Association library. They have a large lending library of English language paperback books donated by members of the community.

TV AND RADIO

A lifesaver to TV junkies has been the arrival of satellite and cable TV. Both have truly revolutionized access to the outside world and TV viewing. Programs that come in over satellite or cable are not censored by the government. You can now get CNN and the NBC

Super Channel. A note, however, to those expecting these programs to be just like those you get at home. They are not, you will be getting the international version of the programs.

Local TV is definitely dreadful for the foreigner. The three local TV stations are government controlled. Two of them (Channels 1 and 3) air mostly Arabic offerings. Channel 2 has daily English language programming, but much of this is censored. Most English programs are either subtitled in Arabic or dubbed.

Local radio stations are similarly rough on the foreigner. English language news can be heard on FM95 at 7:30 a.m., 2:30 p.m., and 8:00 p.m. This is the foreign language station, which broadcasts from 7:00 a.m. until midnight. Besides English language programming, French, German, Greek, and Italian programs are offered. As mentioned earlier, a good option is a short-wave radio receiver. Other options include tape players, boom boxes, and portable CD players. A word of caution with these: bring a good supply of tapes and CDs with you. The ones you find in Egypt are great for local music, but the quality is often inferior. Many are several generations away from any original recording.

NEWSPAPERS AND MAGAZINES

Several options exist for getting printed news in English. Egyptian newspapers definitely slant coverage towards what the government wants to see printed, although some lively debates do appear. Censorship in Egypt is considerably less than in other countries in the Middle East. More than that, there is substantially less censorship in Egypt than ten years ago. President Mubarak has loosened the reigns on the press somewhat, but, if you are expecting all-out freedom of the press, it simply is not there yet.

The Egyptian Gazette is Egypt's daily English language newspaper. Finding the *Gazette* outside of Cairo or Alexandria is problematic. On Saturdays, the edition is called the *Egyptian Mail*. For the past few years, *Al-Ahram* (the Arabic-language daily) has published a weekly English summary on Thursday. Similarly, a French version is published on Wednesday. The *Middle East Times* is a weekly English language newspaper published on Sunday.

Many major Western newspapers and news magazines can be found in Cairo and Alexandria. Some can even be found in other good-sized cities, but they may be a bit dated. Among the English language publications available are *USA Today*, *Newsweek*, and *Time*. These documents are not censored as they are in some other Middle Eastern countries. You can find them at the major hotels, a few newsstands, and bookshops.

Several other magazines are published in Egypt which are rather good:

- *Egypt Today* is a monthly, local English language publication that covers a range of topics. Check out their webpage located at: http://www.egypttoday.com

- *The Middle East Times* is a bi-monthly publication published in the United Kingdom.

- *Egypt Magazine*, a bi-monthly, covers cultural items and contemporary issues.

- *Sports and Fitness Egypt* provides monthly highlights of sporting events.

- *Business Today* is a good magazine for business related topics on Egypt and the world. Check it out at its website: http:/www.arabia.com/EgyptToday

- *Business Monthly* is the monthly journal of the American Chamber of Commerce in Egypt (AmCham). Along with an online version of this journal, the American Chamber of Commerce has an excellent website with lots of information at: http://www.amcham.org.eg

CABARETS AND DISCOTHEQUES

Dancing lights, clinking glasses, and loud music hit you squarely as you step through the doors into the sanctum of Egypt's response to the Western nightclub. Colored lights playing on silver balls bounce kaleidoscope sparkles throughout the room. These are the discotheques frequented by Egyptians.

Everywhere you turn, smiling couples move to the tantalizing tempos of Western disco and rock music. The sounds of the seventies and eighties reverberate through powerful amps blasting from every corner. Hot spots for unmarried Egyptian couples (almost totally upper-class), discos provide a haven of Western style singles' life. You can get imported alcoholic drinks at many clubs, as well as local beer and wine. Dancing is openly flirtatious, though not really suggestive.

Foreigners more frequently patronize another category of nightclub referred to locally as cabarets. These are usually fairly expensive, often including belly dancers, folklore performances, Arabic music, and a lavish food spread. All the major hotels have floor shows and you can usually combine this with an excellent dinner. You will often find cabarets have a cover charge and/or a minimum charge, usually with a tax added on at the end.

CASINOS

Casinos operate in only a few of the five-star hotels in Cairo. Egyptian nationals are prohibited by law from gambling in casinos, but all foreigners are permitted. If you plan to gamble, be sure to make it when you are not out with your Egyptian friends so they won't have to remind you they are not allowed. The casinos have everything from inexpensive slot machines to large-stake gaming tables. You will have to show your passport to get in.

PROSTITUTION, HOMOSEXUALITY, AND EXTRA-MARITAL RELATIONSHIPS

Prostitution is definitely one of those topics most Egyptians do not want to talk about. When pushed, most will simply tell you prostitution is illegal. Some will tell you that they think prostitution used to be legal; others simply tell you there has never been legal prostitution in Egypt. In any event, prostitutes do work in Egypt. Historically, prostitution used to be associated with being out late at night and with the arts – particularly musicians and bellydancers, in other words, those who were outside the mainstream of traditional Egyptian society. The most famous area 40 or 50 years ago used to be around Mohamed Ali Street. Now, there is no organized district, per se, such as in Amsterdam. How do you recognize a prostitute? Again, answers are elusive. Most people answer, "Well, you just know." You probably will, too.

Gay rights do not exist in Egypt. There is no movement, no public acknowledgement for a very simple reason: homosexuality is illegal in Egypt. Homosexual acts leave a person open to being punished for committing the crime of "disgraceful impudent acts." Under this law, a convicted person can be imprisoned for up to one year and fined up to E£300. Usually, this law has not been used against Westerners – they are just deported instead of imprisoned. This does not mean you definitely will be deported rather than imprisoned, however. Recognize this: homosexuality is not welcome in Egypt. Does this mean there are no gay hangouts in Egypt? No, it does not.

As mentioned in other sections, friends of the same sex may hold hands casually in public without this being interpreted as homosexual behavior. But anything that looks like public gestures of affection between persons of the same sex (things that are perceived to be homosexual) provokes strong negative reactions. Men wearing earrings are assumed to be homosexuals!

Messing around with extramarital heterosexual affairs can also result in dealing with the force of the law. A lot of this relates to divorce laws, but laws nevertheless. Does this mean Egyptians don't mess around? No, but be assured that discretion is definitely a must!

The subject of extramarital affairs brings up another topic of interest. What about mixed-gender couples who travel together or live together? This gets a little tricky and there is definitely a double standard. An Egyptian man and woman who are not married to each other cannot register in a hotel room together under the law. On the other hand, usually (though not at all hotels), a foreign unmarried man and woman can register to stay in the same room. But a foreigner cannot register to be in the same room with an Egyptian of the opposite sex if they are not married. So, what do people do? They get separate rooms.

CULTURAL QUIZ

SITUATION ONE

You and your family have been in Cairo for a few months. In a conversation with one of your new Egyptian friends, you express interest in taking your family to visit the beach in Ismailia over the weekend. Your contact tells you, "Oh, I have a lovely villa there which is yours to use. I will arrange everything." On the assigned date, a driver arrives to take you to Ismailia. When you get there, you find that arrangements have been made for a grand meal at a local restaurant. The driver stays in Ismailia to drive you anywhere you want to go while there and then take you back to Cairo the next evening. When you get back to Cairo, you pay the driver for his services and also give him what can be considered a good tip. Next day, you visit your friend to tell him how wonderful the trip was and express your thanks for all the hospitality and use of the villa in Ismailia. He tells you, it was "No problem. You are welcome." Then he tells you that the cost for the trip is E£420. Your response is:

A. "I already paid the driver. Give me a detailed list of the other costs and I will be happy to pay you for that."

B. React with annoyance and shock, and refuse to pay, saying, "Well, where I come from when we invite someone to visit, we don't ask them to pay."

C. Thank him for his gracious hospitality, telling him that this is so little to pay for such a wonderful weekend.

Comment

Well, if you never want to see this friend again, choose either Option A or Option B. If the friend means something to you, choose Option C and write it off to experience. Even though with Option A, you already paid the driver according to your way of thinking, your friend arranged for the driver. Therefore, any money you gave the driver was considered a "tip" by him. Option B is just blatantly insulting to your Egyptian friend.

It is easy to fall into this kind of situation. Your Egyptian friend is not misleading you by offering to arrange everything. They may even suggest you be their guest at their villa, but this still may not mean you would not be expected to pay for the costs. In other situations, especially if your Egyptian friend is quite wealthy, they would not ask you to compensate them for any expenses incurred. In this situation, your friend would assume you would reciprocate on another occasion.

When in doubt, ask. There are a couple of ways to handle this situation beforehand. First, when something like this happens, you could easily tell your friend something like, "Wow, it is great of you to offer. How much do you think it will cost for transportation and everything?" Another way you might want to handle an offer that seems too good to be true or when you don't want to be obligated for a future reciprocation is to say something like, "Oh, I would never presume to impose on you. We would expect to pay for all costs associated with such generosity."

Most of the time, if your friends actually expect you to pay for something, they will be straightforward and treat it as a business deal – especially if you ask. But, don't forget the "rule of threes." Your hosts may first protest that you shouldn't pay. If they do this, be sure to say something like, "Oh, no. I couldn't let you do that much." You should go through this kind of banter until they insist the third time, at which point you can feel free to accept because it means they actually mean you should not pay. Just remember to try to give them an opportunity for a way out since they may feel obligated to offer even if they cannot afford to.

SITUATION TWO

You are responsible for arranging seating for a luncheon meeting for some visiting foreign business people and some Egyptians. Among the twelve Egyptians attending will be the Minister of Important Affairs (fictitious ministry), a distinguished scholar, three prominent business representatives, a university dean, a retired ambassador who advises the prime minister, the consul general assigned to your country, and various other persons. Your home country's delegation will be twelve people, among whom will be: the president and CEO of Conglomerate International, a corporate vice president from another company, the project developer (the person who actually did all the work to make the business deal possible and the person who actually knows the answers to any questions that might be raised), a representative from your country's embassy in Cairo, yourself, and various other persons involved in the deal. How do you seat the people?

    A. Have four tables for six so everyone can sit with their own country's people. They will want to sit with their friends anyway and catch up on the gossip.

    B. Have one long table with seats on each side and let people choose their own seat or assign seats.

C. Place six or eight people from your country at a head table, with the Egyptian contingency down each side along with the others from your country.

D. Arrange for a horseshoe styled table. Seat the three most prominent Egyptians and three most senior people from your country at the head table; alternate the remaining seating between country representatives according to ranking (senior-most ranked persons closest to the head table).

Comment

Well, this one can be difficult because there might be some hidden relative status factors of which you are not aware. Option A is not good because it undermines your intent which is to foster an opportunity for cross-communication between Egyptian and home country people. Option C is equally inappropriate, but for a different reason. Choosing this option suggests that people from your home country are in some way superior to your Egyptian hosts – not the impression you want to give, assuming you want to do business in the country.

Option B is a possible, but better if you direct people to seats either across from or next to a person of similar status. The hazard of letting people choose their own seats is not with the Egyptians (they will undoubtedly assort according to rank), but with your home country participants. Your home country colleagues may well not recognize the importance of status in seating or how their position among the group is perceived. This could easily lead to a low-ranking person sitting next to a very high-ranking Egyptian – after all, who wouldn't want to sit next to a minister, for example.

Option D gives you the best opportunity to recognize important persons from both groups. The tricky part then becomes determining who should sit at the head table. If there is a doubt about who should be recognized in this manner, ask a trusted Egyptian friend. In the example given, the Egyptians you would probably choose to sit at the head table would most likely be the minister, the retired ambassador, and the visiting consul general. Among the visitors, you would probably choose the CEO, the embassy representative and either the project director or the visiting company vice president – depending on how you perceive their importance. Since you are the organizer, you might also seat yourself at the head table, next to the podium so you can easily introduce your speakers.

SITUATION THREE

You decide you want to have a few people over to your house for an informal gathering – just sitting around and talking. One of your favorite friends is a local taxi driver and entrepreneur (on the side). But you really want to have some of your Egyptian business acquaintances, some of whom are professors, over as well to meet some of your home country friends. Who do you invite?

    A. Invite them all over at once. They can all mingle around the punch bowl and buffet. It will be good for your Egyptian friends to meet people from different social strata.

    B. Invite the taxi driver and his family at one time, your business acquaintances at another.

    C. Forget it, just invite foreign friends, it is easier.

Comment

It would not be socially appropriate to invite the taxi driver and business acquaintances at the same time. Choosing Option A would place all of your Egyptian friends in an awkward position and would not change the existing social structure one iota. Choosing Option B is the best choice for being able to share an evening with all of your Egyptian friends. Option C would certainly not insult anyone, but would definitely limit your social circle.

SITUATION FOUR

You are a man doing business in Egypt. Your colleague, Mr. Moustafa, invites you to a meeting at his house for six o'clock on Wednesday evening. When you get there (you are fifteen minutes early), you hear scuffling behind the door and a small voice tells you, "No one is at home."

    A. You scream, "Of course you are home, I hear you."

    B. You try to explain that you have a meeting with Mr. Moustafa at six, but that you are a little early, and insist that you be allowed to come in.

    C. You try reason, explaining that your taxi just left and that it is too hot to wait on the porch.

    D. You tell them who you are and that you will wait on the porch for Mr. Moustafa to come home.

    E. You tell your taxi driver to wait before you go to the door, just in case no one is at home. After being told no one is there, you leave, go have a coffee or tea, and return in thirty minutes to an hour later.

Comment

A, B, and C are definitely bad choices. Responses D or E are acceptable, but probably E is preferable under the circumstances. The reason you got the response you did was because there were only women at home when you called. In this case, it would be inappropriate for you to be allowed into the house. The first mistake was coming early. For one thing, because of the problems with Cairo traffic, Mr. Moustafa may have been delayed in traffic. Alternatively, even though Mr. Moustafa told you to be there at six, he may not really expect you to be exactly on time, much less early. To avoid this kind of situation, a couple of things could be done. First, don't come early. Second, you could stop somewhere close to Mr. Moustafa's house and use a public phone to determine if he is there or you could call before you leave just to reconfirm that Mr. Moustafa will be there when you arrive. In any event, give Mr. Moustafa a little extra time and never challenge the word of the woman answering the door.

SITUATION FIVE

You (a woman) and three of your women friends are out shopping and need a taxi to take you back home. It is a busy time of day and taxis are hard to find.

A. You all decide to get into one small taxi which will hold only three in the back so that one of you must sit in the front seat with the driver.

B. Even though it will cost more and may take more time, you get two taxis, so two can sit comfortably in each one.

C. You decide to wait until you see one of the station wagon-sized taxis. Although you may have to wait for some time and it will cost a little more than one small taxi, a station wagon will allow all of the women to travel together while sitting in a back seat.

Comment

Either B or C is appropriate. Although each of these options is inconvenient and will cost more, they are the better choice because a good Egyptian woman (unless she is very old) would not consider sitting in the front seat with a taxi driver. To do so might invite the driver to make advances to you and could be seen as a sexual come-on.

USEFUL ADDRESSES AND PHONE NUMBERS

FOREIGN EMBASSIES IN EGYPT

At latest count, 118 countries maintain embassies in Egypt. Listed below are some of the embassies which may be of interest to the reader. All are located in the greater Cairo area. The country code for Egypt is 20. The city code for Cairo is 2. E-mail addresses are included where available.

Australia

World Trade Center
Corniche El Nil
Boulak
Phone: 575-0444
Fax: 578-1638
e-mail: austremb@idsc.gov.eg

Canada

6 Mohamed Fahmy El Sayed Street
Garden City
Phone: 354-3110
Fax: 356-3548
e-mail: canademb@idsc.gov.eg

France
29 Giza Street
Giza
Phone: 570-3916; 570-3920

Germany
8 Hassan Sabri Street
Zamalek
Phone: 341-0015
e-mail: germemb@idsc.gov.eg

Ireland
3 Abu El Feda Street
Zamalek
Phone: 340-8264; 340-8547
Fax: 341-2863

Italy
15 Abdel Rahman Fahmi Street
Garden City
Phone: 354-3194; 354-3195
Fax: 354-0657

United Kingdom
7 Ahmed Ragheb Street
Garden City
Phone: 354-0852; 354-0859
e-mail: britemb@idsc.gov.eg

United States of America
3 Lazoughli Street
Garden City
Phone: 355-7371
e-mail: oac@idsc.gov.eg

EGYPTIAN TOURISM OFFICES

Below are listed the Egyptian Tourism Offices located in the four largest cities as well as a few selected offices abroad. Note that some phone numbers contain seven digits, others six. This occurs frequently throughout Egypt.

Headquarters

Misr Travel Tower
Abbassia Square
Cairo
Phone: 285-4509; 284-1970
Fax: 285-4363

Cairo

City code: (02)

Tourist Information	Adly Street	391-3454
Tourist Information	Pyramids	385-0259
Tourist Information	Airport	667-475, ext. 3640
	Int Airport	291-4255, ext. 2223
	New Airport	291-4277
Tourist Information	Railway Station	764-214

Alexandria

City code: (03)

Ramleh Station	Saad Zaghlul Street	807-985
Nuzha	Nuzha Airport	420-2021
Marine Pass. Station	Alex. Port	803-494
Misr Station		492-5985

Luxor

City code: (095)

Tourist Information	Nile Street	382-215
	Luxor Airport	383-294

Aswan

City code: (097)

Tourist Information	Tourist Souk	323-297
Tourist Information	Railway Station	312-811

OFFICES ABROAD

(Country code in parentheses, city code included with phone number)

Europe

FRANKFURT

Agyptisches
Fremdenverkehrsamt
64A Kaiser Strasse
60329 Frankfurt am Main
Germany
Phone: (49) 69-252-319
Fax: (49) 69-239-876

LONDON

Egyptian State Tourist Office
Egyptian House
170, Piccadilly
London w1c9dd, England
Phone: (44) 171-493-5282
Fax: (44) 171-408-0295

PARIS
Bureau du Tourisme, L'Egypte
90 Avenue Des Champselysees
75008 Paris France
Phone: (33) 1-456-29442
Fax: (33) 1-428-93481

ROME
Egyptian Tourist Authority
Bia Bissolati 19
00187 Rome, Italy
Phone: (39) 6-482-7985
Fax: (39) 6-487-4156

Canada
Egyptian Tourist Authority
1253 McGill College, Avenue
Suite 250
Montreal, (Que) Canada H3B2Y5
Phone: (1) 514-861-4420
Fax: (1) 514-861-8071

United States
CHICAGO
Egyptian Tourist Authority
645 N Michigan Avenue
Suite 829
Chicago, IL 60611
Phone: (1) 312-280-4666
Fax: (1) 312-280-4788

LOS ANGELES
Egyptian Tourist Authority
8383 Wilshire Blvd., Suite 215
Beverly Hills, CA 90211
Phone: (1) 213-653-8815
Fax: (1) 213-653-8961

NEW YORK
Egyptian Tourist Authority
630 Fifth Avenue, Suite 1706
New York, NY 10111
Phone: (1) 212-332-2570
Fax: (1) 212-956-6439

South Africa
Egyptian Tourist Authority
First Floor, Regent Place Building
Mutal Gardens
Gradock Avenue
Rosebank
Johannesburg, S. Africa
Phone: (27) 11-880-9602
Fax: (27) 11-880-9604

EGYPTIAN EMBASSIES AND CONSULATES ABROAD

(Country code in parentheses, city code included with phone number)

Australia

EGYPTIAN EMBASSY
1 Darwin Avenue
Yarralumla, Canberra, ACT 2600
Phone: (61) 62-273-4437 / 8

EGYPTIAN CONSULATE – MELBOURNE
124 Exhibition Street, 9th Floor
Melbourne, Victoria 3000
Phone: (61) 3-654-8869 / 8634

EGYPTIAN CONSULATE – SYDNEY
335 New South Head Road
Double Bay, Sydney NSW 2028
Phone: (61) 2-362-3482, 327-5538

Canada

EGYPTIAN EMBASSY
454 Laurier Avenue East
Ottawa, Ontario KIN 6R3
Phone: (1) 613-234-4931

EGYPTIAN CONSULATE – MONTREAL
3754 Cote des Neiges
Montreal, Quebec H3H 7V6
Phone: (1) 514-937-7781

France

EGYPTIAN EMBASSY
56 Avenue díIena
75116 Paris
Phone: (33) 1- 47 20 97 70

EGYPTIAN CONSULATE – PARIS
58 Avenue Foch
75116 Paris
Phone: (33) 1-45 00 84 64

EGYPTIAN CONSULATE – MARSEILLES
166 Avenue de Hamburg
13008 Marseilles
Phone: (33) 91 25 04 04

Germany

EGYPTIAN EMBASSY
Konprinzen Str 2
Bad Godesberg, Bonn
Phone: (49) 228-364-000/8/9

EGYPTIAN EMBASSY – BERLIN
Berliner Str 22
Pankow, Berlin 3
Phone: (49) 30-482-5095

EGYPTIAN CONSULATE – FRANKFURT
Eysseneck Str 52
6000 Frankfurt am Main I
Phone: (49) 69-590-557/8

Ireland

EGYPTIAN EMBASSY
12 Clyde Road
Dublin 4
Phone (353) 1-606-566 / 718

United Kingdom

EGYPTIAN EMBASSY
26 South Street
London W1Y 6DD
Phone: (44) 171-499-2401

EGYPTIAN CONSULATE – LONDON
2 Lowndes Street
London SW1
Phone: (44) 171-235-9777

United States

Embassy of the Arab Republic of Egypt
3521 International CTM.W.
Washington, DC 20008
Phone: (1) 202-895-5400
Fax: (1) 202-224-4319 / 5131

Ambassador's Residence
2301 Massachusetts Avenue, NW
Washington, DC 20008

EGYPTIAN CONSULATE – NEW YORK
1110 2nd Avenue
New York NY 10022
Phone: (1) 212-759-7120

EGYPTIAN CONSULATE – CHICAGO
30 South Michigan Avenue
Chicago, Illinois 60603

EGYPTIAN CONSULATE – HOUSTON
1990 Post Oak Blvd., Suite 2180
Houston, TX 77056
Phone: (1) 713-961-4915

EGYPTIAN CONSULATE – SAN FRANCISCO
3001 Pacific Avenue
San Francisco, CA 94115
Phone: (1) 415-346-9700

INTERNET ADDRESSES OF INTEREST

Probably one of the best sites for finding just about anything on Egypt is: **http://pharos.bu.edu/Egypt/** I almost always go to it first. From this site, you can find a link to almost anything you need.

Another excellent comprehensive site is Egypt's Information Highway at: **http://www.idsc.gov.eg/**

Also see the Official Egyptian Ministry of Tourism Site: **http://touregypt.net/**

Arabic Classes

Offered at several good places in Egypt. Some sites offer more information than others, but try these: **http://www.ili.com.eg/** (International Language Institute); **http://britcoun.org/egypt/** (British Council); and the International Language Institute at the American University in Cairo at **http://inf.auc.eun.eg** or at its North American mirror site at: **http://auc-inf.org/www/main.html**

216

Other Sites

Other useful information can be obtained from the U.S. Department of State's site at: **http://www.state.gov**

For health information specifically on Egypt and North Africa, check the Centers for Disease Control site: **http:/www.cdc.gov.travel/ nafrica.htm** or for more general travel health information see: **http:/ /www.cdc.gov.travel/travel.html**

FURTHER READING

Abu-Lughod, Janet. *Cairo: 1001 Years of the City Victorious.* 1971. Princeton University Press. Out of print, but you may be able to find this in a second-hand bookstore. It remains probably the best history of the development of Cairo.

Arberry, Arthur J. *The Koran Interpreted.* 1964. Macmillan. Many scholars regard this as the most literary English translation of the Qur'an.

Budge, E.A. Wallis. *Egyptian Religion Egyptian Ideas of the Future Life.* 1899 (reprinted in 1972 and 1975 by Routledge and Kegan Paul). You may have difficulty finding this book, but it is worth it if you are interested in ancient Egyptian religion. In particular, this book discusses how ancient Egyptians regarded resurrection and future life. The major source is the collection of religious papyri named the "Book of the Dead." If you are interested in the topic, see also Budge's works entitled *The Book of the Dead* and *Egyptian Magic.*

Dawood, Richard, ed. *Travelers' Health: How to Stay Healthy All Over the World.* 1994. Random House. This book provides practical information of problems encountered by travellers.

Esposito, John. *Islam: The Straight Path.* 1992. Oxford. Put together with Esposito's *Islam and Politics* (Syracuse, 3rd Edition, 1991), you can get a good introduction to Islam and the issues related to modern Islamic activism.

Fakhouri, Hani. *Kafr El-Elow: Continuity and Change in an Egyptian Community,* 2nd Edition. 1987. Waveland Press, Inc. Dry reading in a standard anthropology ethnographic style, but informative. What is important about the information in the book is its analysis of change occurring in an industrial, urban village that has a traditional folk-peasant cultural base.

Fernea, Elizabeth Warnock and Basima Qattan Bezirgan, eds. *Middle Eastern Muslim Women Speak.* 1977 (6th printing 1992). University of Texas Press. Fernea (B.J. to friends) is known for her warmth and humanistic style of writing which gives the reader an in-depth understanding of women throughout the Middle East. This anthology, edited by Fernea and Bezirgan, addresses areas other than Egypt, but has several poignant articles directly related to women in Egypt. Highly recommended for anyone interested in women in the Middle East. Also, try looking at other books written by Fernea (such as *Guests of the Sheikh* or *Women and the Family in the Middle East.* Once you start reading, you will find her work difficult to put down!

Fernea, Elizabeth Warnock and Robert A. Fernea. *Nubian Ethnographies.* 1991. Waveland Press, Inc. For anyone interested in this important subculture within Upper Egypt, the Ferneas' description of life and hardships associated with being Nubian during this century captures your imagination and provides intricate detail on this important group. You will gain exhaustive detail about the Nubian relocation that resulted from building of the Aswan High Dam.

Harris, Philip R. and Robert T. Moran. *Managing Cultural Differences*, 4th Edition. 1996. Houston, TX: Gulf Publishing Company. For those anticipating conducting any international business, this book provides a basis for understanding the nature of cultural differences as they affect business. It has specific sections for the major areas of the world, and one short section specifically addressing Egypt.

Hobbs, Joseph J. *Bedouin Life in the Egyptian Wilderness.* 1989. University of Texas Press. This book is an interesting study of nomadic life among the Bedouins of Egypt. Not nearly as readable as Mahfouz or Fernea, it still provides important information on the beliefs, values, folklore, and ethnobotany of this small group of Egyptians.

Hourani, Albert. *A History of the Arab Peoples.* 1991. Harvard Press. Actually, reading any of the myriad of articles or books written by Professor Hourani will give you an outstanding synthesis of 1,400 years of political, cultural, and social events in the Middle East as well as useful information regarding more specific issues in the region.

Kemp, Barry. *Ancient Egypt: Anatomy of a Civilization.* 1992. Routledge. This book provides an excellent summary of what we currently know and understand about ancient Egyptian culture and society.

Logan, Leanne, Geert Cole, Damien Simonis and Scott Wayne. *Egypt: a Lonely Planet Travel Survival Kit,* 4th Edition. 1996. Oakland, CA: Lonely Planet Publications. Of the basic travel guide books, I like this one best. This book is quite helpful and easy to carry around. It has no in-depth information on the antiquities, but has a wealth of information on places to go and see other than Egypt's ancient past. The maps are all right, but difficult to read.

Mahfouz, Naghib. *Palace Walk.* Naguib Mahfouz was the first Egyptian author to win the Nobel Prize for Literature. Start the Cairo Trilogy with *Palace Walk* and work your way through all three. In addition to these, *Respected Sir* (1986) is an excellent example of his later writing. This book addresses one of the most characteristic features of dealing with contemporary Egyptian life: the labyrinthine bureaucracy. Actually, you will enjoy anything he wrote. His style is clear and you always think you are part of the scene.

Mansfield, Peter. *The Arabs,* revised edition. 1992. Viking Penguin. This is a good, readable introduction to the political and social history of the modern Arab world.

Marsot, Afaf Al-Sayyed. *A Short History of Modern Egypt.* 1985 (reprinted 1994). Cambridge, UK: Cambridge University Press.

For a good general history of Egypt since 1800, read this book. It is a good place to get an initial familiarity with the political and historical forces that shaped contemporary Egypt.

Nydell, Margaret K. *Understanding Arabs: A Guide for Western-ers*.1987. Yarmouth, ME: Intercultural Press, Inc. This book is especially helpful for total newcomers to the cultures of the Middle East. Although most of the examples are general and not specific to Egypt, much of the content applies throughout the Arab speaking world. It is particularly useful as a quick guide for understanding many of the linguistic nuances in the region.

Seton-Williams, Veronica and Peter Stocks. *Egypt: The Blue Guide*. W.W. Norton Co. This is probably the best, in-depth coverage of any of the guidebooks related to Egyptian Antiquities. It includes copious details and maps, but is rather heavy to drag around with you.

Spencer, William. *Global Studies: The Middle East*, 6th Edition. 1996. Dushkin Publishing, U.S.A. This reader is short, sweet, and to the point. It provides a series of articles for understanding events in the Middle East and a country report with pertinent data for each country in the region. Not a hardcore academic's choice, but excellent information.

Waterbury, John. *The Egypt of Nasser and Sadat: The Political Economy of Two Regimes*. 1983. Princeton University Press. This book addresses the socialist transformation of Egypt during the regimes of Nasser and Sadat and discusses many reasons for its failure. If you are interested in political economy, also see Waterbury's other works on the area.

West, John Anthony. *The Traveler's Key to Ancient Egypt*, New Edition. 1995. Wheaton, IL: The Theosophical Publishing House. West presents controversial interpretations of Egyptian antiqui-ties, but interesting in any event. Weighs much less than *The Blue Guide*, but not nearly as comprehensive. Good site maps.

ACKNOWLEDGEMENTS

Much of the data gathered for this book results from directing two field schools in Egypt sponsored by the University of North Texas, Institute of Anthropology and the Study Abroad Program. Special thanks to Dr. David Keitges for helping make these field schools happen. Thanks to all my students who went to Egypt with me. Their remarkable incidences of culture shock showed me that culture shock is not just a long-term response, but one likely to clobber those aware of the phenomenon and who are there for short periods. Their questions and observations reminded me of what Egypt looks like when you are "new" to its environs no matter how "cool" you think you are. A special thanks to Violet Sparks and Michelle Robicheaux for their assistance and support throughout the field schools and subsequently. Also, a special thanks to Cynthia Talbot for suggesting that I write this book. Thanks to all the folks at Times Editions I have neither met nor communicated with, but who worked on this book. Special thanks at Times to Shova Loh for getting me started on the book and to Jonathan Griffiths for his support, rapid e-mail responses, and editorial expertise.

Thanks above all to all the people of Egypt who have been so patient with my questions and who always make me feel welcome. Thanks to Minister Amal Osman (Ministry of Social Affairs) and her staff whose hospitality made possible visits to special schools and NGOs in Egypt. A special thanks to the following, who helped me in more ways than I can think to mention, I am forever in their debt: Ambassador Hussein El Kamel (International Cooperation Advisor, Prime Minister's Cabinet Information and Decision Support Center); Dr. Mahmoud M. Amr (Chair, Department of Occupational Medicine,

Cairo University, Kasr el-Aini School of Medicine); and Mr. Medhat A-Monem (Egypt's greatest tour guide, Aswan). Also, a special thanks to Mr. Mohamed Dahawi; Mrs. Riri el-Aasser; Mr. (soon to be Dr.) Khalid Dahawy; Mrs. Amany Khalil; Mr. Amr Dahawy; Mr. Mortada Mohamed, and Dr. Mohamed El Sayed Salama. My family deserves special recognition for putting up with my absences and erratic schedule. Through it all, they encourage me and it helps. Thanks Mom, Melinda, Jackie, Ed, Darrell, and Tuffy (aka, "The Tuffster")!

THE AUTHOR

S. L. Wilson, Director of Information Synthesis, is a cross-cultural communication and international business consultant who specializes in "how to get things done" in Egypt and the U.S. Wilson has worked as an educator, advisor, negotiator, business consultant, planner, and mediary since 1979. She began working in Egypt in 1987 while serving as a health and human resources delegate to Egypt from the Texas Senate where she was on staff. Since that time, Wilson has continued to actively assist development between Egyptian and American interests. She has written numerous publications, led university based training programs to Egypt, and conducted research in Egypt and the Gulf States. In 1994, she created, organized, and directed a new international field school program conducted in Egypt for the University of North Texas Institute of Anthropology.

Wilson served on the faculties at the University of Texas Southwestern Medical School, the University of Texas Medical Branch at Galveston, and the University of North Texas. Her areas of specialty include:

International Business Communications, Styles, and Negotiations
Managing Cultural Diversity
Peoples and Cultures of the Middle East
How to Develop Cross-cultural Communication Programs
Economic Development Strategies in the Middle East
Public Policy
International Health/Epidemiology
Strategic Planning
Research Methods and Analysis

Wilson holds a B.A. from the University of Cincinnati, Ohio (with honors in Anthropology), and M.A. and Ph.D. degrees from Southern Methodist University in Dallas, Texas.

Her email address is slwegypt@hotmail.com

INDEX